The Booklover's Guide to New Orleans

The Booklover's Guide to New Orleans

SUSAN LARSON

with additional research by

KEVIN McCAFFREY

Louisiana State University Press

Baton Rouge

Copyright © 1999 by Susan Larson
All rights reserved
Manufactured in the United States of America
First printing
00 02 04 06 08 07 05 03 01 99
2 4 5 3 1

Designer: Michele Myatt Quinn
Typeface: Sabon
Printer and binder: Thomson-Shore, Inc.

Library of Congress Cataloging-in-Publication Data:

Larson, Susan, 1951–
    The booklover's guide to New Orleans / Susan Larson ; with
additional research by Kevin McCaffrey.
        p.   cm.
    ISBN 0-8071-2415-X (cl. : alk. paper). —ISBN 0-8071-2416-8
(pa. : alk. paper)
    1. Literary landmarks—Louisiana—New Orleans Guidebooks.
2. Authors, American—Homes and haunts—Louisiana—New
Orleans Guidebooks. 3. New Orleans (La.)—In Literature Bibliography. 4. Bookstores—Louisiana—New Orleans Guidebooks.
5. New Orleans (La.) Bibliography. 6. New Orleans (La.) Guidebooks.
    I. McCaffrey, Kevin.   II. Title
PS267.N49L37   1999
810.9'976315—dc21   99-37833
                                                        CIP

The paper in this book meets the guidelines for permanence and
durability of the Committee on Production Guidelines for Book
Longevity of the Council on Library Resources. ∞

To the happy Wassermans—Julian, Casey, and Dash

and

In memory of Mark Zumpe—a lovely man, a great bookseller

What I love about New Orleans is that it tolerates every kind of eccentricity. Tennessee Williams didn't end up there by accident.

—James Lee Burke

Contents

Illustrations

Illustrations

Acknowledgments

This book would never have been written without the patient insistence of Kathryn Mettelka of the Louisiana Endowment for the Humanities. For that most of all, as well as for a grant from the Louisiana Endowment for the Humanities, a division of the National Endowment for the Humanities, my heartfelt thanks.

At Louisiana State University Press: Gerry Anders (who more than lived up to his reputation as a writer's best friend), Kristin Bryan, Margaret Hart, Maureen Hewitt, Pat Hoefling, Les Phillabaum, Laura Gleason, Michele Quinn, and the happily retired Claudette Price.

Thanks to these wonderful librarians and scholars: at the *Times-Picayune,* Nancy Burris and Danny Gamble, who always go above and beyond; at the Historic New Orleans Collection, Pamela Arceneaux, Jessica Travis (now at the Jefferson Parish Library System), Florence Jumonville (now at the University of New Orleans Earl K. Long Library), and Patricia Lawrence and John Magill, for assistance with photographs.

Thanks to fabulous friends and booklovers: Patricia Brady, for her historian's eye; Marigny Dupuy, for cheerful support; Carol Antosiak and Peg Kohlepp, for research assistance; Kevin McCaffrey, for delightful companionship on early research expeditions; Jon Newlin, for an unsentimental education; Diana Pinckley, for always being there, purple pen and words of advice at the ready; and Christine Wiltz, for the generous gift of knowledge and time taken from her own work.

Finally, from one "grumpy Larson" to the happy Wassermans: my son Dash and daughter Casey, for unbelievable patience and often hilarious distractions, and my husband Julian, for schlepping all those books to and from libraries, for tracking down elusive info, and for knowing this would someday come to an end. This book is for you.

The
Booklover's
Guide to
New Orleans

We were suddenly driving along the blue waters of the Gulf, and at the same time a momentous mad thing began on the radio; it was the Chicken Jazz'n Gumbo disk-jockey show from New Orleans, all mad jazz records, colored records, with the disk jockey saying, "Don't worry 'bout *nothing!*" We saw New Orleans in the night ahead of us with joy. Dean rubbed his hands over the wheel. "Now we're going to get our kicks!" At dusk we were coming into the humming streets of New Orleans. "Oh, smell the people!" yelled Dean with his face out the window, sniffing. "Ah! God! Life!" He swung around a trolley. "Yes!"

—Jack Kerouac, *On the Road*

Welcome

PEOPLE COME TO New Orleans to let the good times roll. They come for food, for music, and for stories—stories they've heard, and stories they've read. They come because they've heard that New Orleans has something special, a culture unique in these United States, resistant to the pressures of time and homogenization. They come because they've heard the siren call of Tennessee Williams and hope to experience the kindness of strangers. Or because they've read *Confederacy of Dunces* and want to taste those Lucky Dogs for themselves. Or because some deep, dark longing for a vampire's caress draws them into the New Orleans night. Perhaps, on a boring drive home through suburban traffic, they've heard the wry, acerbic voice of writer and National Public Radio commentator Andrei Codrescu extolling the uneasy virtues and bountiful contradictions of his hometown. People come to New Orleans for a taste of something—something spicy, something sweet, something they've read or dreamed about. They come filled with desire, ready to be seduced.

And it's easy to fall in love with the Big Easy. Most residents stay in love with it, for better or worse, for life. Most tourists are half in love with the place before they get here. They've seen the picture-postcard views of the French Quarter, dreamed of the Mississippi, heard the clang of the streetcar—thanks to books and movies and music. Even first-time visitors to New Orleans often comment on their feeling of easy familiarity with the city, as if they were stepping into the pages of a well-known and loved storybook or entering a theater or movie set. (Occasionally they are, as movie crews have become a fact of life here.) Visitors are sometimes overwhelmed by a sense of déjà vu, present moments merging with memories of places seen on film or read about in books. These moments when the past collides with the present encapsulate much of the charm of New Orleans. That glorious past—as well as the present urban conflicts that are its legacy—are explored and celebrated in the literary heritage that is one of the city's greatest treasures.

In this book we trace the steps of many famous literary figures, past and present. (As Andrei Codrescu says in his introduction to the anthology *New Orleans Stories: Great Writers on the City*, "If New Orleans went into the memorial plaque business for all the writers who ever lived here they would have to brass-plate the whole town.") There's a calendar of literary celebrations, a reading list to enjoy before you come and after you've gone, and a little bit of lagniappe too. Perhaps, if you're a writer or a booklover, you'll decide to stay a while.

Why have so many writers come to New Orleans?

The earliest European explorers came here three hundred years ago looking for wealth and fame. What they found—and wrote about—was a kind of natural wonderland. Historians and religious figures came later and reported their progress back to the Old World. The clashes of culture—Spanish, French, Creole, African— were grist for the writing mill in what became one of the South's great cultural centers. Journalists came for a visit and reported what they saw, leading others to come and take a look for themselves.

Some writers were drawn here as part of Mississippi River voyages. Samuel Clemens became Mark Twain after a visit to New Orleans; and what would *Life on the Mississippi* be without a stop at this port city?

Others made New Orleans a must-see on grand tours of the American continent. William Thackeray visited the city on his way to St. Louis, stayed at the grand St. Charles Hotel, and said, "At that comfortable tavern on Pontchartrain we had a bouillabaisse than which a better was never eaten at Marseilles." Of course, Thackeray's opinion of the city may have been improved by parting gifts of two bottles of cognac, a dozen bottles of Medoc, and a case of light claret. One for the road indeed!

Gertrude Stein and Alice B. Toklas came to New Orleans as part of their triumphant American tour. There are still locals who remember a party given in their honor, where the two ladies sat side

I liked it all from the first: I lingered long in that morning walk, liking it more and more, in spite of its shabbiness, but utterly unable to say then or ever since wherein its charm lies. I suppose we are all wrongly made up and have a fallen nature; else why is it that while the most thrifty and neat and orderly city only wins our approval, and perhaps gratifies us intellectually, such a thriftless, battered and stained, and lazy old place as the French quarter of New Orleans takes our hearts?

—Charles Dudley Warner, "Sui Generis,"
in *Harper's* magazine

by side on a sofa for two hours and said nothing to anyone else. Finally, Alice turned to Gertrude and said, "Well, Puss, time to go!"

Some native writers stayed here all their lives. Grace King, historian, novelist, literary hostess, and one of the great southern women of letters, experienced Reconstruction in New Orleans and spent her life writing about her beloved city and state in such books as *New Orleans: The Place and the People* and *Balcony Stories*.

Other New Orleans–born writers find time away restorative. Walk through the shady streets of the Garden District to Anne Rice's mansion, where the author lives and works today, spinning her fiercely moral tales of the supernatural, after years in San Francisco. Her sprawling house on First Street is also the setting for the best-selling book *The Witching Hour.*

Some native writers left for good but drew on their childhood memories for the stuff of literature. When Lillian Hellman chronicled her childhood, she returned to the Prytania Street boarding-house run by her aunts, the venue that inspired her play *Toys in*

Gertrude Stein (seated, right) and Alice B. Toklas at the Basement Book Shop during their visit to New Orleans

Historic New Orleans Collection. Acc. no. 1983.215.113

the Attic. The noted *New York Times* book critic Anatole Broyard, also a native, wrote about New Orleans summers in a wonderful essay called "Summer Madness." (When Broyard left New Orleans, he also left behind his racially mixed heritage, revealed to great controversy only after his death.)

Some writers find, as Tennessee Williams did, a spiritual home in the Crescent City. Williams, one of the writers most strongly identified with the city, made it uniquely his own. Every writer who takes New Orleans as a subject does so in the shadow of his evocation of the place.

Some writers came to New Orleans specifically to write. Walker Percy moved here acting upon his decisions to marry, to write, and to become a Catholic. In those early days he lived near Audubon Park. Later he moved to a house on Milan Street, where he began work on *The Moviegoer,* that great New Orleans novel of struggle against despair.

And some writers came to New Orleans to hide out for a while. William S. Porter, a fugitive from embezzlement charges leveled by a Texas bank, fled to New Orleans, went to work for the newspapers, lived in a French Quarter apartment, and wrote several stories set in the city. Porter is better known by his literary alias, O. Henry.

What is it about the city that draws writers? The exoticism? The freedom? The sultry air? The beautiful old buildings steeped in a long and complicated history? Cheap rents and great food?

Perhaps it is living in a place where words—like food, like music—are necessary for life, a place where a writer's privacy is understood and respected. New Orleans is a city where being a writer is, indeed, one of the oldest and most honorable professions.

The literary past is very much alive here. The horse-drawn carriages that convey tourists through the French Quarter often resound with folk history. "And over there, that's where Tennessee Williams lived when he wrote *Streetcar,*" the driver will proclaim, and a reverent hush will fall over the group. Tourists drawn down the seductive little stretch of Pirate's Alley between the Cabildo and St. Louis Cathedral will find themselves in Faulkner House Books, where an elegant store now occupies the space where Faulkner lived and worked during his brief but transformative time in the city.

And the present is equally vital. There are a number of successful and aspiring writers doing good work here; strong independent bookstores; entertaining and educational literary conferences and festivals. All build upon a distinguished literary past and an inviting atmosphere that will always attract the eccentric and the creative.

The city's literary offerings include something for everyone: literary novelists, mystery writers, children's authors, an increasing number of romance writers, and distinguished writers of nonfiction, especially of history and biography.

Those literary offerings are on display at bookstores throughout the city. New Orleans is the home of the New Orleans Gulf South Booksellers Association, which numbers among its members booksellers who specialize in feminist books, African American literature, mysteries and true crime books, general interest books, and fine antiquarian items. Lovers of limited editions will enjoy browsing at Faulkner House Books, while those with less rarefied and expensive tastes will seek out Kaboom Books or Beckham's Book Shop in the Quarter, or George Herget Books on Magazine Street or Great Acquisitions Uptown for used or rare books.

New Orleans also supports literature with its own distinctive, festive flair. There's the Tennessee Williams/New Orleans Literary Festival each spring, with a full weekend schedule of dramatic and literary events. In late spring the New Orleans Jazz and Heritage Festival brings authors to town for work and play; the book tent at the festival features a full schedule of author appearances. Fall brings the Pirate's Alley Faulkner Society's celebration of Faulkner's birthday, as well as the New Orleans Popular Fiction Conference.

Every week year round, literary events in the form of readings and autographings take place throughout the city. Any Sunday afternoon, you can amble into the Maple Leaf Bar, scene of the longest-running reading series in the South, to settle in for a few drinks and hear writers read their latest work. Now that's New Orleans style.

Best of all, literary culture in New Orleans is relatively inexpensive and open to everyone. Take a few extra steps past a writer's house and soak up the atmosphere. Maybe it will inspire you. Visit a bookstore and see what strikes your reading fancy (and budget).

Stop by one of the city's many archives and browse through literary treasures for free. Take a seat at one of the city's many coffeehouses and watch the writer scribbling at the next table.

And listen. New Orleans is telling its stories all the time. Chances are you'll hear some while you wait for the streetcar or stroll down the avenue. So read, walk, enjoy, live. Isn't that why you're here?

The world's most famous streetcar in its pre-retirement days
Historic New Orleans Collection. Acc. no. 1974.25.37.103

The ability of Saxon to laugh at himself was always evident. At a civic function in New Orleans, after one of the speakers in his praise of native writers had been carried away with local pride and Creole exuberance, Meigs Frost turned to Saxon and said: "Well, as I always say, Lyle, so many of us here are internationally famous locally." This became a phrase Saxon often repeated when visitors gushed (as they frequently did) over his works. . . .

. . . *Fabulous New Orleans* and *Old Louisiana* went on selling year after year, and there was always a great demand for Saxon's autograph from visitors who were discovering the city and the state for the first time through his eyes. He was gracious about the autographing, but joked about it. "I started out to be a writer," he would say, "and ended up as a souvenir."

—Edward Dreyer, "And Some Friends of Lyle Saxon," in Saxon's *The Friends of Joe Gilmore*

Tales of the Crescent City

VIRTUALLY EVER MAJOR American city claims a certain literary mystique, some lovely blend of the real and the imagined that draws readers to seek out places they remember from beloved books. To walk in New York City is to see it through the eyes of Edith Wharton, Grace Paley, or Dawn Powell as much as it is to hear the traffic or see the lights of Broadway or the crowds in Central Park. Chicago's Lakeshore Drive, with its grand view and crisp breezes, calls to mind Saul Bellow and Nelson Algren and Studs Terkel. And a reader's trip to San Francisco often includes a pilgrimage to City Lights Books in North Beach, famed home to so many writers, or to the Castro district, part of the gay world immortalized in Armistead Maupin's wonderful *Tales of the City*.

The otherworldly landscapes of Anne Rice or the comic ramblings of Ignatius Reilly are every bit as attractive to tourists as a trip down Bourbon Street or a dinner in a renowned restaurant. Does it matter that the streetcar named Desire has been replaced by a malodorous modern bus? Not really. It's still there to be seen in the mind's eye. Does the French Quarter belong to Tennessee Williams? Anne Rice? William Faulkner? It belongs to all of them, just as certainly as it does to any contemporary resident with one of those coveted courtyards.

For writers, a city can be a touchstone, an inspiration, a scourge, a beloved prison—or all of those things. Every city has libraries and bookstores filled with writings that are rooted in it alone, work that would not have happened or would have turned out differently had it been nurtured somewhere else. In fact and in fiction, every city demands an accounting—including history, commentary on current conditions, interpretations of what is unique, enduring or changing. It is a rare city that can support and inspire as many writers, and for as long, as New Orleans.

A city develops its own literary history and infrastructure—prominent authors whose work defines the place: books that come to represent it in the popular consciousness; histories chronicling its actual events; novels, plays, and poems that interpret its spirit; and the network of bookstores, literary salons and festivals, writers' conferences, educational programs, and media support that energizes successful writers and helps establish new ones.

As a sense of self-awareness develops in a place, people are driven to respond to myriad things that charm and outrage them, to explain and analyze what constitutes the special identity of their locale. The resulting literature has been as varied as human nature. Yet if they occasionally feel the long shadow of well-known writers who have preceded them, writers today are busy casting New Orleans in their own light. And while it is tempting to make literary tradition out of literary history, it's clear that an individual writer's work grows out of a uniquely personal response to a particular place at a particular time.

In the Beginning (1718–1860)

New Orleans has always had its writers, beginning with explorers of the New World, driven to push westward and report their discoveries. The first history of Louisiana, published in 1758, was written by Antoine Simon Le Page du Pratz, who found the place not to his liking and returned to France. Other early accounts include François Xavier Martin's *History of Louisiana*, published in 1827, Charles Gayarré's four-volume *History of Louisiana*, issued from 1848 to 1866 in French and English, and Alcée Fortier's four-volume history of the same name, published in 1904.

Some particularly endearing early writings are those of Marie Madeleine Hachard, a young Ursuline nun who came to New Orleans in 1727 and recorded her impressions in letters to her family, which were eventually published in France. In one she wrote, "There is a popular song sung here which says that this city is as beautiful as Paris. However, I find a difference between this city and Paris. Perhaps the song could convince people who have not seen the capital of France, but I have seen it, and the song does not persuade me to the contrary." Centuries later, writer Hamilton Basso would refer to New Orleans as "Paris in my own backyard," perhaps demonstrating the difference between the immigrant and the native sensibility.

The city's early literature owes its greatest debt, naturally, to the French, particularly the French romantics. After finding it a disappointing investment, France had ceded New Orleans to the Spanish in 1762, taken it back briefly at the start of the 1800s, and sold it to the United States in the Louisiana Purchase of 1803. But the French heritage lingered. (The influence also worked in reverse, as Louisiana fired creative imaginations in the home country; the French writer Chateaubriand, for example, set two novels, *Atala* [1801] and *René* [1802], in the colony.)

By 1850, Charles Testut could include fifty-two writers in his *Portraits Littéraires de la Nouvelle Orléans*. Poets and brothers Dominique and Adrien Rouquette, who lived at 413 Royal Street (you can still see the letter *R* in the wrought ironwork above what is now Moss Antiques), were the best-known writers of this period. Dominique published two collections of poems, *Meschacébéennes* (1839) and *Fleurs d'Amérique* (1856). Adrien became a missionary to the Choctaws, and his best-known work, the novel *La Nouvelle Atala* (1879), grew out of that experience.

After the Civil War, the French influence largely declined. The notable exception was Alfred Mercier, who after his education in France returned to New Orleans to practice medicine and write. His novel *L'Habitation Saint-Ybars* was an important contribution to Louisiana literature, although little read or known today. Mercier was also instrumental in the 1876 founding of the French literary society L'Athénée Louisianais and edited its journal, *Les Comptes-rendus*.

Drawn to this bend in the river, folks just kept on coming—and the words just kept on flowing. The landscape inspired them. The confluence of cultures inspired them. What drew early writers here? The Mississippi River, for one thing; the early days of the French opera here, for another. The exoticism of the place, combined with a steady stream of reporting from visitors, brought journalists to mingle with natives who were making names for themselves in

Our city brought her entire character from France, her qualities, as in French good qualities are politely called, and her defects. But who thinks of her defects without extenuations? Not the Canadian and French pioneers who installed her upon the banks of the Mississippi, imagining thereby to install her upon the commercial throne of America; not the descendants of these pioneers, and most assuredly not those whom she has since housed and loved.

Critical sister cities note, that for a city of the United States, New Orleans is not enterprising enough, she has not competition enough in her, that she is un-American, in fact, too Creole. This is a criticism that can be classed in two ways; either among her qualities or her defects. It is palpably certain that she is careless in regard to opportunities for financial profit, and that she is an indifferent contestant with other cities for trade development and population extension. Schemes do not come to her in search of millionaire patrons; millionaires are not fond of coming to her in search of schemes; noble suitors, even, do not come to her for heiresses. It is extremely doubtful if she will ever be rich, as riches are counted in the New World, this transplanted Parisian city. So many efforts have been expended to make her rich! In vain! She does not respond to the process. It seems to bore her. She is too impatient, indiscreet, too frank with her tongue, too free with her hand, and—this is confidential talk in New Orleans—the American millionaire is an impossible type to her. She certainly has been admonished enough by political economists: "Any one," say they, "who can forego a certain amount of pleasure can become rich." She retorts (retorts are quicker with her than reasons): "And any one who can forego a certain amount of riches can have pleasure."

—Grace King, *New Orleans: The Place and the People*

various literary forms. It's fashionable, every now and then, to speak of a New Orleans literary renaissance, but the truth is, writers have always been here, writing.

And this against all odds. A location below sea level, humid and damp, is never kind to those paper artifacts that are the holy relics of literary culture. Plus, there was the city's reputation as a wild and wicked—and illiterate—place to contend with. From the very beginning, New Orleans was known as for low amusements rather than high culture.

EARLY BOOKSELLING

In an article published in the *Louisiana Historical Quarterly* in 1937, "Books and Booksellers in New Orleans, 1730–1830," writer Roger Philip McCutcheon quotes a French observer's remark in a Paris publication in 1803 that in New Orleans there were "no booksellers either, and for a good reason, that a bookseller would perish of hunger there in the midst of his books, unless these taught the fascinated reader the art of doubling his capital in a year's time."

In the face of such a gloomy view, McCutcheon points out that people were indeed reading in New Orleans, with fifty-six booksellers or stores operating between 1804 and 1824. So prominent a personage as Judah Touro, this city's most famed philanthropist, sold books. In 1816 merchant Vincent Nolte, himself the author of *Fifty Years in Both Hemispheres* (1854) as well as the inspiration for Hervey Allen's novel *Anthony Adverse* (1933), was offering imported books for sale, as were many others. There were reading rooms and rental libraries throughout the city. The first public library was founded in 1808. The French printer and bibliographer Antoine Boimare had a rental library of some 10,000 volumes. The first bookseller advertised himself as Mermet, *"marchand libraire,"* in 1808 and had a shop on Royal St. in 1811.

LES CENELLES

The city's complex racial heritage has always been reflected in its literature. Perhaps the most significant local publication of the

Memorabilia from New Orleans's literary past

Courtesy booksellers Carey Beckham and Alton Cook

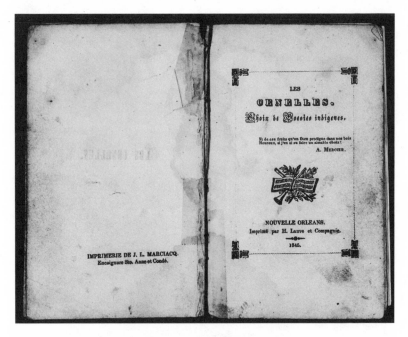

Title page of *Les Cenelles*

Historic New Orleans Collection. Acc. no. P7.632.RL

mid–nineteenth century was *Les Cenelles* (1845). Edited by Armand Lanusse, it was the first anthology of poetry by African Americans to be published in the United States. Containing eighty-two poems by seventeen poets, *Les Cenelles*—"the hawthorns"—grew out of an 1843 magazine called *L'Album Littéraire*. Three of its contributors—Pierre Dalcour, Victor Séjour, and Camille Thierry—received further recognition in France. The book is very rare today (only a few copies are known to exist in the city, in the Historic New Orleans Collection, the Tulane University Library, the Xavier University Library, and one private collection) and commands enormous prices.

VISITING WRITERS BEFORE THE WAR

Although relatively few writers were writing in English in New Orleans before the Civil War, some of them are now extremely well known. John James Audubon earned fame primarily as an artist, but writing was an integral part of his life. The great painter's *Journals* from 1821 and 1822 describe his daily life in New Orleans; he lived in Louisiana from 1821 to 1830. His residences included 706 Barracks Street and 505 Dauphine Street; Audubon Park bears his name. He spent some time at Oakley Plantation as a tutor to a family's young daughter; at least one writer is working on a novel about that period in Audubon's life.

Walt Whitman wrote for the *New Orleans Crescent* in 1848, and his "I Saw in Louisiana a Live Oak Growing" is perhaps the greatest poem associated with the state. The place on Washington Avenue where Whitman stayed no longer exists, but you can follow the avenue (past the contemporary landmark of Commander's Palace, just off Prytania Street), enjoying the magnificent live oaks, down to the river and imagine what he saw there.

Samuel Langhorne Clemens traveled to New Orleans frequently between 1857 and 1861 as a young riverboat pilot and—according to at least some of his biographers—acquired his pen name, Mark Twain, here. He described his early piloting experiences and a later journey down the river in *Life on the Mississippi*.

THE CENTENNIAL EXPOSITION OF 1884

A golden age of literary activity began in the late 1800s, initiated partly by such visitors as Edward King of *Scribner's,* who came to New Orleans in 1873. The single greatest influx of men and women of letters occurred with the New Orleans world's fair—officially, the "World's Industrial and Cotton Centennial Exposition"—in 1884. Joaquin Miller covered the fair for New York papers, Julia Ward Howe headed the fair's Women's Department, and editors Richard Watson Gilder of *Century* magazine and Charles Dudley Warner of *Harper's* arrived to take in the extravaganza and absorb the local culture. These visitors and others like them provided important links to the larger world of New York publishing, thereby offering new opportunities for New Orleans writers, increasing readers' interest in the city, and engendering more demand for pieces about it. Many names from this period have endured; some are enjoying a critical revival and reassessment, George Washington Cable, Lafcadio Hearn, and Grace King among them.

CABLE, KING, HEARN, CHOPIN ET AL.

Cable's tales of Creole life gained national attention after his short story "'Sieur George" was published in *Scribner's* magazine in 1873. Though Cable, a native New Orleanian, has often been dismissed as a local-color writer, a new generation of readers is now discovering the city through his eyes as his works are reprinted. Many French Quarter buildings—for example, Madame John's Legacy and Lafitte's Blacksmith Shop—are exactly as he described them more than a century ago, only now they are burnished by their association with his work. His Garden District home was a popular destination for visiting writers.

Cable's books include *Old Creole Days, The Grandissimes, Dr. Sevier,* and the nonfiction work *The Creoles of Louisiana.* Then as today, New Orleanians dislike criticism, even from within, and especially when they recognize the truth of it. As an early civil rights activist, Cable inspired a storm of outrage, so much so that he moved to Northampton, Massachusetts, where he continued to associate with the literati of his day and wrote a charming little book, *The Amateur Garden,* in which he described with sweet nostalgia the gardens of New Orleans in winter.

Grace King's career as a writer began in direct response to Cable's popular success and his depictions of racial injustice. In the course of becoming a Creole apologist, she also became one of New Orleans's great women of letters. Her 1886 short story "Monsieur Motte" is still taught today. Some of her other well-known works are *Balcony Stories* (1892), *New Orleans: The Place and the People* (1907), and *The Pleasant Ways of St. Medard* (1916). King's elegant mansion on Coliseum Square was occupied by members of her family until recently.

One of the most interesting chroniclers of New Orleans during this period was the romantic, enigmatic, and prognathously ugly Lafcadio Hearn. Born in the Greek isles to an Irish father and a Greek mother, raised in Greece, Ireland, Britain, and France before

Lafcadio Hearn

Historic New Orleans Collection. Acc. no. 1974.61.10

immigrating to America, he arrived in New Orleans in 1877 from Cincinnati and lived here for ten years. Hearn wandered about the city, watching (though he was blind in one eye), reporting, and taking part in the life of the place. He captured unique aspects of Creole life and dialect because, as an outsider, he was open to them. (After having left behind his wife, a woman of color, he was rumored to have had an affair with Marie Laveau.) He recognized the value of Creole culture and sought to collect and preserve its stories.

During his decade in New Orleans, Hearn produced remarkable writing for local newspapers—he was the first literary editor of the *Item* and he wrote for the *Times-Democrat*. He is the author of such Louisiana classics as the novel *Chita* (1889) and *"Gombo Zhebes"* (1885), a collection of Creole proverbs he gathered on his peregrinations throughout the city, recently republished by Temperance Hall Press. A food lover, Hearn also opened a restaurant on Dryades St. called Hard Times and wrote *La Cuisine Creole*, as

19

well as one of the guidebooks to the 1884 Centennial Exposition. He eventually settled in Japan, where he became a cult figure in the city of Matsue; he spent the rest of his years writing about Japanese culture for an American audience. (Today Matsue and New Orleans, bound by their shared adoptive son, are sister cities.) A recent critical biography, *Wandering Ghost,* by Jonathan Cott, has led to a Hearn revival, but as long ago as 1949, Malcolm Cowley called Hearn "the writer in our language who can best be compared with Hans Christian Andersen and the brothers Grimm."

Kate Chopin's works were rediscovered with the feminist movement's search for literature reflecting women's experience, and *The Awakening* is now taught as an American classic. Chopin lived in New Orleans from 1870 to 1879, and much of her time here was occupied with her duties as a wife and mother. She spent summers on Grand Isle, where the dramatic conclusion of *The Awakening* takes place. She also resided for a time in the north Louisiana plantation country of Cloutierville and Natchitoches, although most of her life was spent outside Louisiana. Her experience in New Orleans is the basis for most of her published work. Strollers on Esplanade Avenue can still see Creole cottages like Edna Pontellier's home in *The Awakening.* Chopin lived the relatively privileged life of the wife of a cotton factor (broker for rural planters), but she was quick to see the strictures of New Orleans society and to envision another, more liberated existence for women.

Two writers of children's books are also associated with New Orleans during this period. Ruth McEnery Stuart was not a New Orleans native, but she wrote two stories for children set here, *Solomon Crow's Christmas Pockets* (1896) and *The Story of Bagette* (1902). Cecilia Viets Jamison lived in New Orleans from 1887 to 1902. Her three children's books—*Lady Jane* (1891), *Toinette's Philip* (1894), and *Thistledown* (1903)—are still cherished possessions in many New Orleans households.

Mollie Moore Davis came to New Orleans in 1879; her husband was the editor of the *Daily Picayune.* She wrote primarily novels, short stories, and plays. In a charming little book, *Keren-happuch and I,* published in 1907, she told stories about the famous guests at her salon on Royal Street—Eugene Field, Booth Tarkington, Lafcadio Hearn. George Washington Cable, and Grace King among them.

Alice Moore (better known as Alice Dunbar-Nelson), who grew up in Uptown New Orleans, published her first book, *Violets and Other Tales*, in 1895. She married poet Paul Laurence Dunbar and, in New York City, knew many of the leading members of the Harlem Renaissance. A second collection of her short stories, *The Goodness of St. Rocque*, was published in 1899. Dunbar-Nelson was rediscovered in the 1980s when scholar Gloria Hull edited her diary, *Give Us Each Day: The Diary of Alice Dunbar-Nelson*, as well as her collected works.

Poetry and Advice in the Newspaper

New Orleans newspapers, in the nineteenth century as today, nurtured and provided employment for writers. Eliza Jane Poitevent, who grew up on a plantation near Pearl River, Louisiana, became the literary editor of the *Daily Picayune* in late 1860 at the weekly salary of $25. She was the first woman on the staff, and she married editor Colonel A. M. Holbrook in 1872. When he died, she took over the paper herself, becoming the first woman publisher of a daily city newspaper in the U.S. She married newspaperman George Nicholson in 1878. (The Nicholson family owned the newspaper for another eighty years.) She wrote poetry under the pseudonym Pearl Rivers, and under her editorial leadership poems began to appear occasionally on the *Daily Picayune*'s front pages. She hired her friend Elizabeth M. Gilmer, whom she knew from summer vacations in Bay St. Louis, Mississippi, to come to work at the paper. Gilmer would gain national fame as a journalist and advice columnist, writing under the pseudonym Dorothy Dix.

O. Henry Hides Out

Always, New Orleans has seemed like a great place for writers to hide out. Perhaps one of the earliest to do so was William Sydney (sometimes Sidney) Porter, who came here on the lam from embezzlement charges in Texas. He insisted he got his pen name,

O. Henry, here, but no one quite knows how. He wrote four stories with New Orleans settings—"Blind Man's Holiday," "Cherchez la Femme," "Renaissance at Charleroi," and "Whistling Dick's Christmas Stocking." ("Hostages to Momus," the first story published under the O. Henry pseudonym—which Porter sometimes claimed to have discovered in the society column in a New Orleans newspaper—sounds very local but in fact mentions the city only in passing.) Porter lived in a rooming house, now a restaurant, at 241 Bourbon St., and hung out with reporters at a place in the Quarter called the Rookery.

THE *Double Dealer* AND THE TWENTIES

The next notable period in New Orleans literary history began in the 1920s, when the renowned literary journal the *Double Dealer* launched its five-and-a-half-year run under the editorial leadership of Albert Goldstein and Julius Friend. It began as a response to H. L. Mencken's criticism of the South as a "Sahara of the Bozart." In a 1951 essay for *Dixie Roto Magazine* (part of the *Times-Picayune States*), after *Dealer* contributor William Faulkner had received the Nobel Prize, founder Albert Goldstein recalled the magazine's origins:

"Four young men—Julius Friend, John McClure, the late Basil Thompson, and I—had put our heads together and dreamed up an ambitious project. We conceived a serious literary magazine. Its chief aim was to encourage budding writers; incidentally, it would show critic H. L. Mencken, at that time plagued with the notion that the South was culturally stagnant, that he didn't know what he was talking about." Youth and lack of funds were no obstacles for the determined editors, and as Goldstein wrote, what "started as 'A Magazine for the Discriminating,' soon became 'A National Magazine from the South.' "

Sherwood Anderson, already firmly established in America's literary pantheon, attached himself to the *Double Dealer* crowd and wrote an article for the magazine, ambitiously entitled "New Orleans, the *Double Dealer,* and the Modern Movement in America." The essay celebrates the city and Anderson's experience in it: "I am

Front cover of the *Double Dealer,* October 1921

Courtesy the author

in New Orleans and I am trying to proclaim something I have found here and that I think America wants and needs."

Some of his words seem eerily applicable to the present: "At any rate, there is the fact of the 'Vieux Carre'—the physical fact. The beautiful old town still exists. Just why it isn't the winter home of every sensitive artist in America, who can raise money enough to get here, I do not know. Because its charms aren't known, I suppose. The criers-out of the beauty of the place may have been excursion boomers." Of course, Anderson may have been especially charmed by his own apartment in the Pontalba Buildings, those lovely structures bordering two sides of Jackson Square and named for Micaela Almonester, Baroness Pontalba, who oversaw their construction in the mid–nineteenth century.

Anderson's residency in 1922 and 1924 attracted other writers to New Orleans, including the young Faulkner. Other visitors to Anderson's apartment included John dos Passos, Carl Sandburg, Gertrude Stein, and Anita Loos. Anderson spent his first winter in New Orleans working on *Many Marriages* and *Horses and Men*.

Defiantly literary (and financially unsuccessful), the editors of the *Double Dealer* sought out and published some of the most remarkable names in American—and New Orleans—literature. William Faulkner's and Ernest Hemingway's first published work appeared in the *Double Dealer*.

Goldstein writes, "Dig into the old files and you find Faulkner, Hemingway, Thornton Wilder, Mark Van Doren, Richard Aldington, Gilbert Seldes, Ben Hecht, Mary Austin, Louis Untermeyer, William Alexander Percy, Howard Mumford Jones, Robert Penn Warren, John Crowe Ransom, Edmund Wilson, Ezra Pound, Burton Rascoe, Jean Toomer, Robert Graves, Lola Ridge, Henry Bellamann, Lord Dunsany, Allen Tate, Maxwell Bodenheim, Carl Van Vechten, Hamilton Basso, David Cohn, Llewlyn Powys, Witter Bynner, Elizabeth Coatsworth, and dozens more of that ilk."

The editors achieved their goals and even convinced Mencken that, as Goldstein put it, the magazine was "delivering Southerners from what he called their cultural swamp.

"After nearly six years of publication—a long life as 'little' magazines went—the *Double Dealer* was discontinued. Not because it had failed; to the contrary. It had been a constructive force in the postwar movement which sought to kick over the traces of a decayed literary tradition. It bowed out mainly because its work was done."

Its editors and writers went on to other things; John McClure became the editor of *Scribner's* magazine, providing an important link from New Orleans to the New York publishing world.

Even in its heyday, the *Double Dealer* was not the only game in town. Other writers were at work on other projects in New Orleans in the 1920s. Roark Bradford began his fourteen years here as a newspaper reporter but eventually turned to fiction. *Ol' Man Adam an' His Chillun* was the basis for Marc Connelly's 1929 play *The Green Pastures,* which won the Pulitzer Prize for drama in 1930. That same year another Quarterite, Oliver La Farge, received the Pulitzer Prize for fiction for his novel *Laughing Boy.*

La Farge taught at Tulane with the noted archeologist Frans Blom and took his meals with William Faulkner and the artist William Spratling in their French Quarter apartment on Pirate's Alley. At the same time, Hamilton Basso, a New Orleans native, was beginning his long career as a journalist and novelist (he is perhaps best known for *The View from Pompey's Head,* published in 1954). Today Basso's books are being reissued, and he is the subject of a new biography.

Faulkner, who lived in the city for six months in 1924 and 1925, wrote articles for the *Times-Picayune* and the *Double Dealer* that were eventually published as *New Orleans Sketches.* Later works with New Orleans settings were the novels *Mosquitoes,* a wicked satire of Quarterites on a boating expedition on Lake Pontchartrain; *Pylon,* based on the opening of the Shushan Lakefront Airport; and *Soldier's Pay.*

Many who knew Faulkner in his New Orleans days remember him as an unpleasant little man who drank a lot and kept an observant eye on everyone. That eye became all too obvious in a little book published in 1926 called *Sherwood Anderson and Other Famous Creoles.* Faulkner collaborated with his roommate Spratling on this work, which consisted mostly of caricatures by Spratling and captions by Faulkner. One representative example was "Oliver LaFarge, from Harvard, a Kind of School Near Boston," indicating, as Spratling put it, "Bill's lack of respect for Yankee culture." The final caricature depicts the two collaborators, complete with empty bottles under the writer's chair and the BB gun the two friends would occasionally fire from their window at French Quarter passersby (even nuns, Spratling says in his autobiography). The first edition of this little curiosity is now very rare and expensive, though the book has been reissued by the University of Texas Press.

In August 1928, Zora Neale Hurston, of Harlem Renaissance fame, came to New Orleans and began collecting folklore from, among others, friends and disciples of the voodoo priestess Marie Laveau, who died in 1881. Hurston stayed in New Orleans and in Algiers (across the Mississippi) for the winter, and came back from October through December of the following year. Her work here is collected in *Mules and Men,* published in 1935.

THE WPA AND THE THIRTIES

Literary activity continued at a high pitch in the 1930s with the Federal Writers Project, a New Deal WPA program designed to provide employment for writers and artists. In Louisiana the project was led by the remarkable Lyle Saxon. Saxon, "Mr. French Quarter," was a seminal figure not only in literature but in historic preservation. In October 1935 he became the state director of the Federal Writers Project in Louisiana; later he served as regional consultant for projects in other southern states (the program ended in 1942). Among the important works produced by the project in Louisiana are *The New Orleans City Guide* (1938), *The Louisiana Guide* (1941), and *Gumbo Ya-Ya* (1945), a folklore collection that is still a local best seller.

Saxon asked Marcus Christian, the "poet laureate of New Orleans Negroes," to direct the Negro unit—separate in those days of segregation—of the Federal Writers Project. Christian succeeded the project's first director, Lawrence Reddick, a Dillard history professor. From 1936 to 1943 the group included Octave Lilly, Elizabeth Catlett, Arna Bontemps, Benjamin Quarles, and Margaret Walker. Novelist Frank Yerby, who later wrote *The Foxes of Harrow,* was also a professor at Dillard at that time. *The History of Black Louisiana* in manuscript (it was never published in book form) is part of the Marcus Christian Collection at the University of New Orleans, along with many poems, including Christian's epic, Whitmanesque "I Am New Orleans."

A wonderful era in New Orleans bookselling began in 1928 when Tess Crager opened her Basement Book Shop in the 7700 block of St. Charles Avenue. The store was moved in 1932 to 7221 Zimple Street, where it remained for fifty years. Crager and her husband, Robert Crager, formed a publishing company in 1947 and published John Chase's landmark history of New Orleans street names, *Frenchmen, Desire, Good Children,* as well as reprinting the work of Lyle Saxon. Tess Crager was the agent not only for Saxon but also for New Orleans authors Charles "Pie" Dufour, John Chase, and Robert Tallant. Authors who visited the store over the years included André Maurois, Edna St. Vincent Millay, Gertrude Stein, W. H. Auden, Stephen Spender, T. H. White, and Alexander Woollcott.

Katherine Anne Porter lived in the lower Pontalba Apartments on Jackson Square in 1937; she was in love with and later married Albert Erskine, business manager of the *Southern Review.* Robert Penn Warren and his wife rented a room around the corner on Royal Street so they could come down from Baton Rouge, where Warren was managing editor of the *Southern Review,* and visit her on weekends.

The Forties and Fifties

Two playwrights associated with New Orleans received national acclaim in the era of the 1940s and 1950s. Lillian Hellman's *The Little Foxes* was produced in 1939 and followed by *Another Part of the Forest, Watch on the Rhine,* and *Toys in the Attic;* the latter's setting was based on the Prytania Street boardinghouse of Hellman's aunts. Tennessee Williams won Pulitzer prizes for *A Streetcar Named Desire* in 1948 and *Cat on a Hot Tin Roof* in 1955.

Novelist Frances Parkinson Keyes led an active literary career from the 1920s to the 1970s, but her most famous novel, *Dinner at Antoine's,* was a best seller in 1948. Newspaperman Harnett Kane enjoyed a long career writing about Louisiana; he was such an active promoter of his work that an *unsigned* book of his is a rarity today.

The beat generation made a brief early foray into New Orleans in 1948 and 1949, when William S. Burroughs was living in Algiers, drawn to the drugs and decadence of the city. Jack Kerouac and his on-the-road sidekick and muse Neal Cassady visited Burroughs in 1948.

In the mid-1950s Maxine Cassin founded the *New Orleans Poetry Journal* and the New Orleans Poetry Journal Press, whose first book was Vassar Miller's *Adam's Footprint,* published in 1956.

THE SIXTIES AND SEVENTIES

The 1960s and 1970s were a time of intense and diffuse literary activity in New Orleans. Writer Jon Webb moved back here with his wife, Gypsy Lou Webb, in 1954 (the Webbs had lived in New Orleans about 1940, when Jon was writing his first book, *Four Steps to the Wall*). He determined to publish a magazine called the *Outsider* in 1960. Poet Walter Lowenfels provided an introduction to Henry Miller, and the first issue included the work of such beat icons as Gregory Corso, Lawrence Ferlinghetti, Allen Ginsberg, and Gary Snyder. The four issues of the *Outsider* are now collector's items. The Webbs' Loujon Press also produced exquisite editions of work by Miller, Ginsberg, and Charles Bukowski.

The Free Southern Theater, founded by John O'Neal and Gilbert Moses and originally based in Mississippi, moved to New Orleans in 1964. Tom Dent, son of Dillard University president Albert Dent, returned to New Orleans from New York in 1965 to continue his career as a poet, playwright, and activist. With Kalamu ya Salaam, the theater established a writing workshop, BLKARTSOUTH, which began publishing a journal in 1968. That journal, *Nkombo,* included work by such contemporary writers as Quo Vadis Gex-Breaux, Nayo (Barbara Malcolm), Dent, ya Salaam, and Norbert Davidson. The Congo Square Writers Workshop was begun in 1972 by Dent and Lloyd Medley.

Another literary circle revolved around the *New Orleans Review,* based at Loyola University and founded by Miller Williams (who wrote the poem for President Clinton's 1996 inauguration) and short-story writer and novelist John William Corrington. The *New Orleans Review* first appeared in 1969 and continues to the present; it published the first chapters of John Kennedy Toole's *Confederacy of Dunces.*

Other literary reviews included the *New Laurel Review,* founded by Paul and Alice Moser Claudel in 1972 and still published periodically under the editorial direction of Lee Meitzen Grue. The *Xavier Review,* begun in 1961 as *Xavier University Studies,* is now published annually (after ceasing publication from 1971 to 1980) and has contained writing by Al Young, Tom Dent, and Jerry Ward, and others, as well as interviews with Alex Haley, Ernest Gaines, Walker Percy, James Baldwin, and Andre Dubus.

Shirley Ann Grau, a graduate of New Orleans's Newcomb College who turned to writing after Tulane would not accept her as a graduate student, won the Pulitzer Prize for fiction in 1965 for her novel *The Keepers of the House.* Walker Percy won a National Book Award for *The Moviegoer* in 1962. Percy, for many years a

A New Orleans publishing party in 1969; from left,
Walker Percy, Kay Archer, T. Harry Williams,
Turner Catledge, Tess Crager, and Paul Rossiter

Historic New Orleans Collection. Acc. no. 1983.215.28

The Maple Street Book Shop soon after its opening (above) and today. Current owner Rhoda Faust is the young woman with very long hair.

Top photo by Marty Pitts; bottom photo courtesy the Maple Street Book Shop

kind of elder statesman for young writers, encouraged Sheila Bosworth and Nancy Lemann in their work. He taught a small class at Loyola in 1976 that included such writers as Tim Gautreaux, Kenneth Holditch, Walter Isaacson, and Valerie Martin. (Ironically, during this same period, John Kennedy Toole was teaching at nearby Dominican College but would never meet Percy, who eventually saw Toole's work through to posthumous publication.)

In 1970, a banner literary year for the region, Louisiana State University historian T. Harry Williams won both a Pulitzer Prize and a National Book Award for his biography *Huey Long*, Lillian Hellman won a National Book Award for her memoir *An Unfinished Woman*, and former New Orleanian Robert Stone won a National Book Award for his novel *Dog Soldiers*. New Orleans native Anne Rice, then living in San Francisco, became a best-selling novelist with *Interview with the Vampire*, published in 1976.

The Maple Street Book Shop, founded by Mary Kellogg and her sister Rhoda Norman in 1966, and now owned by Kellogg's daughter, Rhoda Faust, is still a haven for local authors and prominently identified with several of them, including Ellen Gilchrist and Walker Percy. George deVille opened his elegant double-decker bookshop on Carondelet Street in 1977. One of the country's oldest gay bookstores, Faubourg Marigny Book Store, was founded by Tom Horner in the mid-1970s and is now run by Alan Robinson.

LITERARY NEW ORLEANS TODAY

The 1980s and 1990s saw an extraordinary rise in the profile of New Orleans writers and New Orleans literary culture. The 1980s started out strong when literary recognition came to several New Orleanians in 1981. John Kennedy Toole won a posthumous Pulitzer Prize for *Confederacy of Dunces*, and Ellen Gilchrist received a National Book Award for *Victory Over Japan: A Book of Stories*. *Confederacy of Dunces*, one of the greatest of all New Orleans novels, captured the imagination of the country with its outrageous protagonist and its hilarious yet realistic portrayal of life in New Orleans, far beyond the stereotypical Garden District elegance and French Quarter decadence.

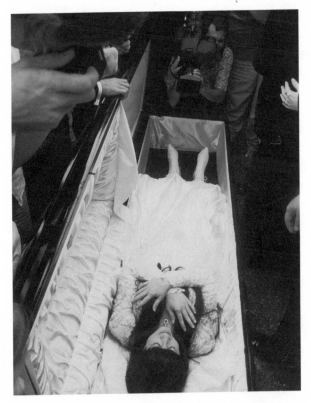

Anne Rice living it up at her jazz funeral

Courtesy New Orleans Times-Picayune, *photo by Bryan Berteaux*

In addition to awards, several wide-ranging factors contributed to the consolidation of the city's literary reputation.

Each literary era requires its own prominent figures. Often these writers work in more than one genre, and some go on to make connections in the larger literary world. That network, in turn, can benefit their local contemporaries. Consider how the reputations of Charles Gayarré, George Washington Cable, Lafcadio Hearn, Grace King, Sherwood Anderson, and Lyle Saxon drew writers to the city during earlier periods.

Today such figures include Shirley Ann Grau, Anne Rice, and Richard Ford. The achievements of other Louisiana authors—among them Stephen Ambrose, Robert Olen Butler, Ernest Gaines, and James Lee Burke—also help to raise the city's literary standing. By supporting local events, employing the city as a setting, or simply, as in the case of Richard Ford and Stephen Ambrose, by keeping the city as a home base, speaking *from* if not *for* New Orleans, these writers contribute to the city's literary reputation.

Of course, it does not hurt that, in addition to being good writers, some of these key figures also possess compelling personalities. Anne Rice and Richard Ford are both newsworthy in entirely different ways. When Ford wins a literary award, it reflects well on his hometown. When Rice arrived at one of her book signings closed in a coffin on a horse-drawn hearse, staging her own jazz funeral, the press was certainly on hand to cover the event. Both are willing and able to engage the public in a variety of settings. Both receive significant exposure in the national media.

In the 1990s several important commentators on history and politics have had strong New Orleans ties. Historian Stephen Ambrose, who founded the Eisenhower Center for American Studies at the University of New Orleans, wrote highly regarded biographies of Presidents Eisenhower and Nixon, achieved bestsellerdom with his *D-Day, June 6, 1944,* and followed that up with the popular successes of *Undaunted Courage: Meriwether Lewis, Thomas Jefferson, and the Opening of the American West* and *Citizen Soldiers.* His authoritative presence and mastery of his subject matter have led television journalists and producers to seek his thoughts on subjects ranging from Nixon's funeral to the D-Day anniversary and the film *Saving Private Ryan.*

Historian Douglas Brinkley, Ambrose's successor at the Eisenhower Center, has written on everything from the United Nations to his innovative approach to teaching history through travel, chronicled in *The Majic Bus.* Currently engaged in writing a multivolume biography of Jimmy Carter, Brinkley has also worked with the network C-SPAN in creating a holistic approach to teaching history in concert with literature.

Three influential observers of the national scene are New Orleans natives. Walter Isaacson, author of the 1992 best seller *Kissinger,* is now the managing editor of *Time* magazine. Nicholas Lemann achieved a huge success with *The Promised Land: The*

Great Black Migration and How It Changed America. Michael Lewis, who made a fortune on Wall Street, chronicled his adventures in the best-selling *Liar's Poker,* followed by a collection of his financial journalism in *The Money Culture* and a comic account of the Bush/Clinton presidential race in *Trail Fever.*

Perhaps the most colorful modern-day political commentator/ participant to come out of Louisiana is James Carville, who engineered President Bill Clinton's successful 1992 campaign. He is the author of *We're Right and They're Wrong* and . . . *And the Horse He Rode in On: The People vs. Kenneth Starr,* and coauthor, with his wife, political consultant Mary Matalin, of *All's Fair: Love, War, and Running for President.*

The popular success of some of its works naturally helps to spotlight a literary community. Perhaps the most obvious example is Tennessee Williams's *Streetcar Named Desire.* Thanks to his remarkable portrayal of New Orleans on stage and in film, Williams may have been the world's best-known contemporary playwright. Anne Rice attained bestsellerdom with her Vampire Chronicles, but the film *Interview with the Vampire* brought her even greater national attention. Ellen Gilchrist and Andrei Codrescu have both become familiar to large and loyal audiences with their broadcasts on National Public Radio.

Some writers become local legends; tales of despair and excess abound. The suicide of John Kennedy Toole, author of *A Confederacy of Dunces,* is a case in point. His genius, unappreciated during his life, and his tragic, despairing end became a cautionary tale for every aspiring writer. Toole's story captured national attention, largely through the indefatigable publicity efforts of his mother, Thelma Ducoing Toole.

In 1989, New Orleans lost Everette Maddox, poet and founder of the Maple Leaf Bar's Sunday reading series, to complications arising from alcoholism. Another promising young writer, Seth Morgan, son of Frederick Morgan, founder of the *Hudson Review,* came to New Orleans to finish his novel *Homeboy* and to recover from drug and alcohol abuse. He died in a motorcycle crash in 1990.

Paradoxically, what is bad for a city can be bread and butter for its writers. As New Orleans's real-life crime problem grew in the 1980s and the 1990s, so did its crop of mystery and thriller writers. Julie Smith won the Edgar Award for *New Orleans Mourning,* her first New Orleans–set mystery. The book introduced police detective Skip Langdon during a Mardi Gras murder, and Smith has continued the popular series. Christine Wiltz chose to write from the viewpoint of male detective Neal Rafferty in an edgy, sexy series that began with *The Killing Circle.* (Wiltz also wrote one of the most important novels of contemporary race relations in New Orleans, *Glass House,* published in 1994.)

Several recent series have featured African American detectives, written by white writers. John William Corrington and Joyce Corrington began a promising series with *So Small a Carnival,* told from the viewpoint of an African American detective named Rat Trap. James Sallis, who has written in many genres, achieved his greatest commercial success with the Lew Griffin series, featuring a detective who is also a literature professor. Xavier University librarian Robert Skinner has created the Wesley Farrell series, set in 1930s New Orleans.

Tony Fennelly's Matt Sinclair series employs a gay antiques dealer as the protagonist, while Jean Redmann, who works with NO/AIDS Task force, has created a series centering around a lesbian detective named Micky Knight. At least two local attorneys have turned their hands to fiction: Tony Dunbar writes the Tubby Dubonnet series, with its emphasis on shady dealings and serious gourmet food, and Peggy Woodward writes legal thrillers. Former engineer Laura Joh Rowland creates literary mysteries set in seventeenth-century Japan, while Kevin Allman sets his in Hollywood. Many other mysteries written by non–New Orleanians use the Crescent City as a backdrop. (Not only in mysteries, but in other genres, New Orleans often inspires writers who have never lived here for any significant length of time—and whose lack of experience and research is sometimes reflected in mistakes in their work.)

Contemporary New Orleans writers are working in best-selling as well as literary fiction and nonfiction of every conceivable variety. There are many mystery writers and romance writers, as well as literary novelists. There is an ongoing dialogue between natives and outsiders. And there are a number of observer/participants, people who take part in the culture and report on it. Many writers are creating work that is strictly of local interest, but there are many, many others whose work, inspired by the character of the city, reaches a larger audience.

Beyond providing writers with material and a milieu for their characters, a city can reinforce its writing community through many kinds of public events and programs. The Tennessee Williams/New Orleans Literary Festival debuted in the spring of 1987, and attendance has grown steadily every year since. In recent years the festival has expanded its offerings to include the French Quarter Literary Conference, an opportunity to take master classes with writers. The Jazz and Heritage Festival each spring presents an opportunity for booklovers to meet writers in the festival's book tent. The Pirate's Alley Faulkner Society celebrates Faulkner's birthday each year, presenting awards for new writing in its William Faulkner writing competition. In recent years, the society has added an event called Words and Music: A Literary Feast in New Orleans, which includes a writers conference and musical performances.

Writing courses and workshops throughout the year are sponsored both by local universities and by writing groups such as SOLA (the south Louisiana chapter of the Romance Writers of America) and the Society of Children's Book Writers and Illustrators. The creative writing program at the University of New Orleans is filled to capacity, and students at the city's arts high school, the New Orleans Center for Creative Arts, routinely win national recognition for their literary achievements.

The hope of recognition motivates professional writers as well, of course, and besides the prizes already mentioned, writers associated with New Orleans continued to receive official acclaim for their work in an extraordinary spate of national awards in the 1990s.

Robert Olen Butler received the 1993 Pulitzer Prize and was nominated for the PEN/Faulkner award for *A Good Scent from a Strange Mountain*. His first story collection and eighth book explores the lives of Vietnamese immigrants in south Louisiana, particularly in an area of eastern New Orleans known as Versailles.

Richard Ford, who makes his home in the French Quarter, received both the 1996 PEN/Faulkner and the Pulitzer Prize for his novel *Independence Day* and has appeared at both the Tennessee Williams Literary Festival and the Faulkner Festival.

Louis Edwards, a Lake Charles native, set his most recent novel, *N: A Romantic Mystery,* in New Orleans, painting the city in the dark shades of the noir tradition in film and literature. He is the recipient of a Whiting Writers Award.

New Orleans native John Gregory Brown, now the head of the creative writing program at Sweet Briar, won the prestigious Lyndhurst Prize. He is the author of two critically acclaimed novels set in New Orleans in the 1930s, *Decorations in a Ruined Cemetery* and *The Wrecked, Blessed Body of Shelton Lafleur.*

The story of African American writers in New Orleans has yet to be written, but Kalamu ya Salaam, poet, playwright, essayist, and producer, and poet Brenda Marie Osbey are working to remedy that. Violet Harrington Bryan is the author of a groundbreaking study, *The Myth of New Orleans in Literature: Dialogues of Race and Gender.*

What New Orleans Offers Writers (and Readers)

In an increasingly homogeneous environment, New Orleans still offers a sense of a place unique in itself, a place out of the mainstream and quite happy to be there (local boosterism and casino gambling to the contrary). There's a lot of history here, a lot of tradition. With the rich mix of African American, Catholic, and Creole culture, the foibles of Uptown society, the colorful and complex social rituals of Mardi Gras and voodoo, there's always something to write about.

The city is a place to fill the senses—the eye, with the pleasures of architecture and exotic flora; the taste buds, with food like no other city; the ear, with the lively sounds from jazz to hip-hop. There's the stimulation of a multiracial environment. There are

On New Year's Eve 1999, Felicity strolled through the French Quarter in full view of tourists, freaks, shades, cops, barkers, hustlers. . . . It was drizzling, and lights glowed from every window. The clip-clop of the mules pulling tourist carriages over the cobblestones was muted, as if someone had wrapped their hooves in cotton. Old men walked home in the mist with baguettes sticking out of their brown bags like phalluses. Black generals of a nonexistent African kingdom, resplendent in gold epaulets, brass buttons, silver braids, and chef's hats, stood outlined in the doorways of restaurants, distributing menus to tourists. Mimes, tappers, and hustlers were at work in their customary spots on the sidewalks. And of course, the blue notes of a horn spilled from a recessed doorway. . . .

Her senses were keen. She could smell fresh beignets and chicory coffee from Cafe du Monde; rosemary baked chicken from Irene's; wet dog leading blind (and blind-drunk) beggar; crawfish and crab bisque out of Tujague's; sweaty tourist; dry cumin, bay leaf, pepper, and prosciutto plus olive salad at the Progreso grocery; cigars and newsprint from Sidney's Newsstand; muleshit; roasting coffee at Kaldi's; vanilla scented hooker, spent firecrackers, beer, rotting crawfish. By the time she walked the length of Decatur, she had worked up an appetite.

In front of Dead Star Books, a crowd of cadaverous youth dressed in black crinoline waited sullenly for Angelique Risotto, the queen of gothic. Her novels of bloodsucking had a huge following of pale, listless death lovers. She owned lots of real estate, including numerous churches, behind which she garaged the hearses that took her to book signings. The release of a new book was typically celebrated by an appearance in a coffin carried by pallbearers, from which she would leap in a red wedding dress. . . . Felicity crossed the street to give them a wide berth.

—Andrei Codrescu, *Messiah*

universities and libraries and a reasonable cost of living. Best of all there are places to walk, and around certain corners, a sense of mystery to be explored.

Every year, new writers emerge from New Orleans. Every year new writers come to New Orleans. Some would be writers no matter where they lived; others are writers because New Orleans has in some way inspired, supported or changed them. Many devote themselves to celebrating and analyzing the complex culture around them. Some succeed beyond their wildest dreams; some fail utterly.

Local book wholesaler Joe Arrigo, who's seen writers come and go in his thirty years of selling books here, said once, "Everyone in New Orleans is either writing a book or has an idea for one."

For the past four years now I have been living in Gentilly, a middle-class suburb of New Orleans. Except for the banana plants in the patios and the curlicues of iron on the Walgreen drugstore one would never guess it was part of New Orleans. Most of the houses are either old-style California bungalows or new-style Daytona cottages. But this is what I like about it. I can't stand the Old World atmosphere of the French Quarter or the genteel charm of the Garden District. I lived in the Quarter for two years, but in the end I got tired of Birmingham businessmen smirking around Bourbon Street and the homosexuals and patio connoisseurs on Royal Street. My uncle and aunt live in a gracious house in the Garden District and are very kind to me. But whenever I try to live there, I find myself first in a rage during which I develop strong opinions on a variety of subjects and write letters to editors, then in a depression during which I lie rigid as a stick for hours staring straight up at the plaster medallion in the ceiling of my bedroom.

Life in Gentilly is very peaceful.

—Walker Percy, *The Moviegoer*

Literary New Orleanians:
Where the Writers Are and Were

ONE OF NEW ORLEANS'S greatest charms is the diversity of its neighborhoods, from the otherworldliness of the French Quarter to the studied elegance of the Garden District, to the variety of architecture and culture on Uptown streets, to the slower pace of Carrollton and the suburban sprawl beyond. Writers live in every part of the city.

In this chapter, a list of "Writers and Their Neighborhoods" gives general locations for various writers, while more-detailed information is found under the individual authors' names in the "Literary New Orleanians" section. The only addresses provided are historical ones (as we all know, writers need their privacy to live and work), except for Anne Rice's properties, which are so well publicized—and well secured—that they are included here. But we can give you an idea of what neighborhoods, if not specific spots, appeal to contemporary writers these days.

The French Quarter has always drawn a diverse crowd. Recent residents have included Andrei Codrescu, Richard Ford, and Lindy Boggs, ambassador to the Vatican and author of the memoir *Washington through a Purple Veil* (and whose Bourbon Street house once was home to Thornton Wilder).

The vitality of nearby Tremé, with its strong African American culture and history, has drawn such writers as Tom Dent and Lolis Eric Elie.

The Garden District has been home in the past to such luminaries as George Washington Cable; today its most famous literary resident is Anne Rice, whose mansion at First and Chestnut is the setting for much of her fiction, as well as a frequent destination for tourists.

It's an odd sensation to recognize in oneself the need to be in a particular physical environment, when one longs for the home ground no matter how terrible the memories it holds, no matter how great the efforts made to leave it behind. So I have left this city again and again and thought myself lucky to escape its allure, for it's the attraction of decay, of vicious, florid, natural cycles that roll over the senses with their lushness. Where else could I find these hateful, humid, murderously hot afternoons, when I know that the past was a series of great mistakes, the greatest being the inability to live anywhere but in this swamp? I can't do without those little surges of joy at the sight of a chameleon, of a line of dark clouds moving in beneath the burning blue of the sky. I am comforted by the threatening encumbrance of moss on trees, the thick, sticky plantain trees that can grow from their chopped roots twenty feet in three months, the green scum that spreads over the lagoons and bayous, the colorful conversation of the lazy, suspicious, pleasure-loving populace. I don't think I will leave the city again.

—Valerie Martin, *A Recent Martyr*

A number of writers grew up or have lived Uptown, including Rick Barton, Jason Berry, Ellen Gilchrist, Walter Isaacson, Nancy Lemann, Nicholas Lemann, Michael Lewis (who has said that he and Nicholas Lemann often joke about the "State Street School of Writers," for the neighborhood where the two of them grew up), Valerie Martin, Anne Rice, and Christine Wiltz. Shirley Ann Grau lives in old Metairie; poet Peter Cooley lives in Jefferson.

Who can say what draws a writer to a neighborhood? A love for a house or apartment? The view from a window? A spot on a Mardi Gras parade route? A favorite coffee shop around the corner? Access to a streetcar line? Every New Orleans neighborhood offers its own charms.

A word of caution: Only a few of these sites are open to the public. For most of them, you'll simply have to be content with a glimpse of the exterior.

LITERARY WALKING TOURS

Literary walking tours are available through Heritage Tours, led by former University of New Orleans English professor Kenneth Holditch (504) 949-9805, FAX (504) 948-7821. Call for group or individual rates; minimum of three people per tour. Three tours: a general tour, a Tennessee Williams tour, and a William Faulkner tour; all last approximately two hours. Tours are also available through the National Park Service.

WRITERS AND THEIR NEIGHBORHOODS

French Quarter

Nelson Algren
Sherwood Anderson
John James Audubon
Hamilton Basso
Roark Bradford
Gwen Bristow
Charles Bukowski
Truman Capote

Winston Churchill
John Dos Passos
William Faulkner
Edna Ferber
Eugene Field
Charles Gayarré
Lafcadio Hearn
Zora Neale Hurston
Frances Parkinson Keyes
Oliver La Farge
Clarence John Laughlin
Malcolm Lowry
William March
John McClure
Vincent Nolte
Katherine Anne Porter
William Sydney Porter (O. Henry)
Adrien and Dominique Rouquette
Lyle Saxon
Jon and Gypsy Lou Webb
Thornton Wilder
Tennessee Williams

Garden District

George Washington Cable
Joaquin Miller
Anne and Stan Rice
Edward Larocque Tinker

*Lower Garden District
and Coliseum Square*

Grace King
Seth Morgan
Henry Morton Stanley

Uptown

Stanley Clisby Arthur

Kate Chopin
Dorothy Dix
F. Scott Fitzgerald
Lillian Hellman
Harnett Kane
Sinclair Lewis
Walker Percy
Robert Tallant
John Kennedy Toole

Central City

Lafcadio Hearn

Algiers

William S. Burroughs
Jack Kerouac

LITERARY NEW ORLEANIANS

Nelson Algren (1909–1981)

Algren's *Walk on the Wild Side,* published in 1956, was a picaresque novel of the bohemian life in New Orleans in the 1930s. When drifter Dove Linkhorn hopped a freight and arrived in the city, that moment reverberated all the way to the contemporary rock music scene, inspiring Lou Reed's song of the same name. "That was how Dove came at last to the town that always seems to be rocking. Rocked by its rivers, then by its trains, between boat bell and train bell go its see-saw hours.

"The town of the poor-boy sandwich and chicory coffee, where garlic hangs on strings and truckers sleep in their trucks. Where mailmen wore pith helmets and the people burned red candles all night long in old-fashioned-lamps."

Linkhorn hangs out with the lost souls near the station, "where every window framed some love bird lamed in flight. Where every screen door was a cage. What had been Storyville was now an aviary."

"It was have a ball and spend it all—'Daddy, buy me one more drink and do just what you want with me.' That was what they called fun on old Perdido Street."

Linkhorn also explores the "wonder of Canal," the "nests" along both sides of South Basin, the tastes and smells of the French Market. He hangs out at the corner of Calhoun and Magnolia and ventures along the Tchoupitoulas Street wharves.

Algren, like his character, Fort, "wasn't deluded about New Orleans," and like many visiting writers, did certainly rearrange geography, but his evocation of the city's wicked pleasures lingers still.

Stephen E. Ambrose (1936–)

Illinois native Ambrose came to New Orleans in 1960 to teach at the University of New Orleans. One of America's best-known historians, he is the biographer of Presidents Nixon and Eisenhower, and the author of such bestselling works of military history as *Band of Brothers; D-Day, June 6, 1944: The Climactic Battle of World War II; Citizen Soldiers; The Victors;* and *Undaunted Courage: Meriwether Lewis, Thomas Jefferson, and the Opening of the American West.* Currently, he divides his time between homes in Bay St. Louis, Mississippi and Montana. He is the president and founder of New Orleans's D-Day Museum.

Berthe Amoss (1925–)

A New Orleans native and the mother of six sons, Amoss is a children's book writer and illustrator. She is the author of many illustrated books for children, most recently *The Cajun Gingerbread Boy* and *Five Fairy Tale Princesses,* as well as many novels for young adults. She is the coauthor, with Eric Suben, of two books about the craft of writing and illustrating children's books. She has taught at Tulane University and from 1980 to 1991 wrote a column about children's books for the *Times-Picayune.* She lives Uptown.

Sherwood Anderson (1876–1941)

The Pontalba Building apartment at 540-B St. Peter Street, where Anderson stayed in 1924 with his third wife, Elizabeth Prall Anderson, was designated a Literary Landmark by the Friends of the Library USA in 1997.

By the time Anderson arrived in New Orleans, *Winesburg, Ohio* had already assured his place in American letters. He worked on *Dark Laughter* while he was living here, and the city inspired one of his best-known short stories, "A Meeting South." In it, Anderson describes taking Faulkner to meet a former madam, Aunt Rose Arnold, literally one of the Quarter's most colorful characters. More than six feet tall with bright red hair, she was a survivor of the famed red light district, Storyville. Arnold lived at 625 Chartres.

The Andersons had many famous guests, including Faulkner, Carl Sandburg, Ring Lardner, Edmund Wilson, and Horace Liveright. Anderson had an important influence on Faulkner, Ernest Hemingway, and Gertrude Stein and was generous supporter of young talent. When Anderson's wife asked him to help Faulkner find a publisher for *Soldier's Pay*, he agreed—on the condition that he not have to read it first. Later he and Faulkner fell out after Faulkner mercilessly parodied his mentor in the 1926 book of caricatures *Sherwood Anderson and Other Famous Creoles,* one of the great literary curiosities in the city's history.

Anderson and his wife also owned the house at 715 Governor Nicholls but never actually lived in it.

Stanley Clisby Arthur (1880–1963)

Arthur, a director of the Louisiana State Museum, lived Uptown at 1309 State St. He wrote a biography of John James Audubon and many other books, including *Old New Orleans* and *Louisiana Tours. Old New Orleans* was recently reprinted and is still a delightful guide to the city, not to mention *Famous New Orleans Drinks and How to Mix 'Em,* still in print. Arthur's wife, Ella Bentley Arthur, wrote the children's book *Sonny Boy's Day at the Zoo* (1918) and *Songs of a Creole City.*

John James Audubon (1785–1851)

The naturalist and bird painter arrived in New Orleans January 7, 1821, and wrote in his journal, "at New Orleans at last." He lived at first in a $10-a-month room at 706 Barracks St. between two grocery stores. He supplemented his income by painting human portraits, including a nude portrait of a certain Madame André, who was displeased with the results and proceeded to improve upon the painting herself. In June 1821, Audubon left for Oakley Plantation near St. Francisville, where he had been engaged to tutor fifteen-year-old Eliza Pirrie. After his relationship with the family deteriorated (the artist was a terrible flirt and there was some question about the quality of his tutoring), he returned to New Orleans in October, rented the house at 505 Dauphine St. in the Quarter, and waited for his wife, Lucy, and family to join him. In spring of 1822 he departed for Natchez, leaving his wife behind as a governess and helpmate to a local family until she rejoined him there in the fall. He passed through New Orleans two more times: in 1830 when he and Lucy set sail for England and in 1837 when he was traveling along the Gulf Coast.

James Baldwin (1924–1987)

James Baldwin's stepfather, David Baldwin Sr., was a New Orleans clergyman. James Baldwin himself made several appearances here for Congress of Racial Equality in 1963. He was also a friend of Tennessee Williams during the playwright's Actors Studio years in New York.

Wilton Barnhardt (1960–)

Every word of Wilton Barnhardt's 1993 novel *Gospel* was written in the apartment building on Esplanade Avenue where John Dos Passos once lived. "I turned on the word processor January 2, 1990," he says. "I moved to New Orleans because I knew that's where the book was going to end. And I had to move where I could see the sun and eat the food." Perhaps only Barnhardt would have the audacity to write a novel about a search for a lost gospel and end it with Louisiana as the Promised Land. The North Carolina native is also the author of *Emma Who Saved My Life* and *Show World*.

John M. Barry (1947–)

Journalist John Barry remembers his first glimpse of the Mississippi River, when he was a college student visiting New Orleans for Mardi Gras. His preoccupation with the river led to one of the most absorbing works about it, *Rising Tide: The Great Mississippi Flood of 1927 and How It Changed America* (1997). Barry currently divides his time between the French Quarter and Washington, D.C. He is also the author of *The Ambition and the Power,* about the rise and fall of House Speaker Jim Wright, and *The Transformed Cell: Unlocking the Secrets of Cancer,* written with Dr. Steven Rosenberg. He is a former assistant football coach at Tulane, which "my wife tells me is probably still the high point of my life."

"When I first came to New Orleans, I realized that Tennessee Williams was writing from life," Barry says. "And when I first encountered the New South, in North Carolina, I realized that Walker Percy was writing from life."

Fredrick Barton (1948–)

New Orleans native and UNO English professor Fredrick Barton is the author of *The El Cholo Feeling Passes; Courting Pandemonium; With Extreme Prejudice;* and (with composer Jay Weigel) the musical play *Ash Wednesday.*

Barton grew up in Gentilly and now lives Uptown. He writes, "Contradictory New Orleans is not a place easily summarized and its rich complexity makes it fascinating, haunting, troubling. It's a city in the South but never really of the South. The people are an ethnic polyglot—Africans, Caribbeans, Italians, Irish, Hispanics, Vietnamese—the accents as varied as the people. This is a city with beautiful boulevards straddling grassy esplanades that wind past pockets of poverty as hopeless as those anywhere in the world. The living is easy in New Orleans, the music never out of earshot. The party never stops and that's both wonderful and disturbing. People smile quickly here, but ancient hatreds smolder on. Wilfully decadent New Orleans defiantly refuses to purify, while it stubbornly, joyfully second-lines with hope."

Hamilton Basso (1904–1964)

The New Orleans native grew up over a shoe factory in the 1200 block of Decatur St. His family moved from the French Quarter across Canal Street to the city's American section when he was nine. Basso attended Warren Easton High School and went to Tulane for law school, although he dropped out to work as a newspaper reporter in New York and New Orleans. He married a New Orleanian, Etolia Moore Simmons, who edited the anthology *The World from Jackson Square.* The couple lived in North Carolina and New York, where Basso wrote for the *New Republic, Time,* the *New Yorker,* and *Saturday Review.* Basso is the author of *Beauregard, the Great Creole* and three novels with New Orleans settings: *Relics and Angels, Cinnamon Seed,* and *Days before Lent. The View from Pompey's Head,* published in 1954, was his first best seller.

Jason Berry (1949–)

New Orleans native Berry is a journalist and nonfiction writer. He is the author of a classic work of New Orleans music history, *Up from the Cradle of Jazz,* as well as *Lead Us Not into Temptation: Catholic Priests and the Sexual Abuse of Children; Amazing Grace: With Charles Evers in Mississippi;* and *Spirit of Blackhawk: A Mystery of Africans and Indians.*

"I live in New Orleans because it entertains me," he said in an interview, "a shabby rococo tropical stage for the human comedy writ large. The progression of my residences has gone from Annunciation to Napoleon and Liberty, Jefferson Avenue, unto Belfast Street—from Irish Channel mysteries to the French Revolution, the author of U.S. democracy, thus to hope for peace in Ireland. All of this fits my personality. I love the city for its music, the spiritual imagination, the neighborhoods and ethnic overlays. It's a raw town politically but nothing cosmic happens here which softens my edge of guilt for having passed up a big media stake in DC or New York."

Sheila Bosworth (1948–)

Novelist and playwright Bosworth, a native New Orleanian, was educated at Sacred Heart and Newcomb College, settings that appear frequently in her novels *Almost Innocent* and *Slow Poison.* She now lives in Covington, just north of Lake Pontchartrain.

I remember that Camp Street was treeless, our part of it, and dusty with windswept dirt from tiny yards where grass died in the sun. Camp Street was planted instead with telephone poles, whose black cables roped off block after block; it was as ugly a place in a morning's spring rain as on a winter afternoon. The university section of New Orleans, with three different colleges within its boundaries, was veined with neighborhoods like ours: quiet, still Caucasian, but running dangerously close to the Negro slums past Magazine Street, toward the river. Blue-collar men and women shared the narrow alleyways between double houses with blue-blooded newlyweds, the progeny of the city's oldest families: young interns, unseasoned lawyers, junior stockbrokers, who served out their lean years in thirty-six-month spans and moved on, to the deep lawns of State Street or the wrought-iron balconies of the Garden District. The porch sitters of the poorer streets, the twenty- and thirty-year residents, became accustomed to the occasional sight of the slow-moving, low-slung car, tanned young mother and pink-and-white child inside. "Look!" the mother would cry, holding Baby up to see, "That's the half-a-house we rented the year you were born! You can't remember, can you, sitting in your playpen on that upstairs porch!" Then the young man behind the steering wheel would stop the car and get out, shading his eyes with his hands, staring. "For Christ's sake. Whoever lives there now has let the place go to ruin. How much could it cost them to at least slap on a coat of paint?" A few minutes more, and they would drive on, rolling up their windows, reminiscing about their bittersweet stay in Poverty. They were like rescued shipwreck victims, returning briefly to their desolate island to ponder the happy impermanence of hardship. As for the porch sitters, they acquired, through the years, a certain working knowledge of things. They could quote the price of painting, and decide when to let things go to ruin, and identify at a glance Privilege, as in the blue-eyed child who lived above them for a time, somersaulting in his playpen on an upstairs porch.

—Sheila Bosworth, *Almost Innocent*

Bosworth writes with care and elegance about the world of New Orleans society, its complex mores and history.

Roark Bradford (1896–1948)

Bradford lived in the old Pontalba Building while working as a night editor and then as Sunday editor of the *New Orleans Times-Picayune.* He and his wife, Mary Rose, had a literary salon at their French Quarter home at 719 Toulouse St. and frequently entertained such visiting literary guests as Sinclair Lewis, John Steinbeck, and William Faulkner. Bradford wrote novels and short stories based primarily on his contacts with blacks. He was the author of the popular *How Come Christmas* and his *Ol' Man Adam an' His Chillun* was later adapted as Marc Connelly's 1930 Pulitzer Prize–winning play *The Green Pastures.* Today most of his work is available only in expensive scholarly reprint editions. He died in 1948 of a disease contracted while traveling in West Africa. His ashes were temporarily interred until his son, Richard, came of age five years later; then they were scattered over the Mississippi. Richard lived here until the late 1960s and is himself the author of several novels, the best known of which is *Red Sky at Morning.*

Patricia Brady (1943–)

Brady, who for many years served as vice president for programming for the annual Tennessee Williams/New Orleans Literary Festival, is also the director of publications for the Historic New Orleans Collection. She came to New Orleans in 1961 to attend Newcomb College, and says that she has "always lived Uptown. I have to be close to the Tulane Library. When I come in from the airport, down the River Road to turn onto St. Charles under that canopy of oaks, I always think, 'Oh, I'm Uptown.' I love it that you can have beautiful gardens and be 15 minutes from the heart of the city." In addition to her writing about New Orleans, she is the editor of *Nelly Custis Lewis's Housekeeping Book* (1982), wrote the introduction to the 1983 reprint of *The WPA Guide to New Orleans,* and edited *George Washington's Beautiful Nelly: The Letters of Eleanor Parke Custis Lewis to Elizabeth Bordley Gibson, 1794–1851.*

Douglas Brinkley (1960–)

Brinkley, a Georgia native who grew up in Ohio, is director of the Eisenhower Center for American Studies at UNO and a regular commentator on National Public Radio. He is the author of *The Unfinished Presidency: Jimmy Carter's Quest for Global Peace* and *The American Heritage History of the United States*, both pub-

Roark Bradford's house on Toulouse Street
Historic New Orleans Collection. Vieux Carré Survey Sq. 61

lished in 1998, as well as books on James Forrestal, Dean Acheson, and Franklin Delano Roosevelt. He is the coauthor, with Stephen Ambrose, of *Rise to Globalism: American Foreign Policy since 1938.* He is also the author of *The Majic Bus: An American Odyssey,* based on an innovative and interactive traveling program of teaching American history and culture.

Brinkley came to New Orleans in 1993, lured here by the opportunity to work with Stephen Ambrose. "I came down and loved it." When Brinkley first moved here, he lived on Spain Street near UNO's Lakefront campus, then on Julia St. in the Warehouse District, and now divides his time between a home in Bay St. Louis and an apartment in the French Quarter.

"As an American historian, I've always loved New Orleans because of the river," says Brinkley. "It's dripping and drenched in fascinating American history. And as a boy growing up in Georgia and Ohio, Andrew Jackson was a boyhood hero of mine and his exploits in the Battle of New Orleans created a great sense of excitement for me."

Gwen Bristow (1903–1980)

Bristow (whose married name was Gwen Bristow Manning) was born in South Carolina. A novelist, poet and journalist who reported for the *Times-Picayune,* she lived at 627 Ursulines St. in the Quarter. She was best known for her murder mysteries and historical novels.

Poppy Z. Brite (1967–)

Brite, a rising star in horror fiction *(Lost Souls; Drawing Blood; Exquisite Corpse),* is a native New Orleanian. She dropped out of the University of North Carolina to write her first novel and never looked back. She also ventured into nonfiction with her 1998 biography of rock star and actress Courtney Love; the two met in New Orleans.

"I came back in 1993," Brite says, "but my father had stayed here and I always came back to visit quite a lot. It's always felt very much like my hometown. It's where my earliest memories are from. Some of those memories have inspired my writing to this day. I have these early memories of going to the French Quarter with my parents—all the back alleys and little shops, and the cemeteries, not going inside them, but seeing them from the freeway, like little cities. What I love about New Orleans now is the juxtaposition of beauty and decay which is also such a large part of my work. And I love the indigenous culture, the food and music."

John Gregory Brown (1961–)

Brown grew up in a large Catholic family in New Orleans and attended Tulane. His two novels, *Decorations in a Ruined Cemetery* and *The Wrecked, Blessed Body of Shelton Lafleur,* are set against the background of the 1930s and 1940s and explore family conflicts, Catholicism, and racial dilemmas. He received the prestigious Lyndhurst Prize in 1993. He now lives with his wife (novelist Carrie Brown) and their three children in Virginia.

Charles Bukowski (1920–1994)

The son of an American soldier and a German woman, Bukowski was born in Germany but came to America with his family when he was three and grew up in California. Rebelling against his strict and abusive father, Bukowski was determined to write. He became known for his gritty poems detailing the wonders and problems of ordinary daily life, as well as for his autobiographical fiction demonstrating his sense of alienation from the American mainstream. His poetry seems to prefigure that of the beats, many of whom he knew and many of whom admired him. He worked at countless menial jobs (including a stint at the post office) and was a hard-drinking, hard-living character known for his love of the racetrack.

Bukowski visited New Orleans briefly in 1942 and was struck by the reality of the Jim Crow laws when he boarded a bus and headed for the back, only to be admonished by the conductor. Later, the city would become very important to him when Jon and Gypsy Lou Webb began printing his work in their magazine the *Outsider* (the first issue, published in 1961, had a six-page centerpiece called "A Bukowski Album"; the third issue, published in 1963, was devoted primarily to his poetry); the Webbs' Loujon Press also published collections of his poetry, *It Catches My Heart in Its Hands* (1963) and *Crucifix in a Deathhand* (1965). Bukowski later said that most of the poems for *Crucifix* "were written during one very hot, lyrical month in New Orleans in 1965." Jon Webb honored him with the title Outsider of the Year for 1962, which gave Bukowski no end of pleasure.

The Webbs also introduced Bukowski to novelist and poet John William Corrington, who wrote the foreword to *It Catches My Heart in Its Hands*. The two writers later had a bitter argument that some say ended their friendship, although they continued to correspond for quite some time. In one of his final letters to Corrington, after Corrington had failed to reply to a request to return the letters Bukowski had written to him over the years, Bukowski referred to him sarcastically throughout as "Southern Gentleman."

Barbet Schroeder's 1987 film *Barfly* was based on Bukowski's life.

William S. Burroughs (1914–1997)

It seems inevitable that one of the great literary outlaws of the twentieth century would spend some time in New Orleans. William S. Burroughs—a Harvard-educated child of privilege who migrated to the fringes of society, a drug addict, a homosexual, and a lover of firearms—best known for his hypnotic and hallucinatory books *Naked Lunch* and *Junkie* and his script for the movie *Blade Runner*, lived at 509 Wagner St. in Algiers during 1948 and 1949. He came to New Orleans after being arrested in Texas for public indecency and drunk driving but fared no better here. He cruised Lee Circle and Exchange Alley, at the time notorious drug hangouts, and was arrested for possession—ironically, because the police recognized his companions, Pat and Cole, junkies now remembered only for their connection with Burroughs. Burroughs fled to Mexico rather than stand trial in New Orleans and face a two-year stint in Angola Penitentiary.

Jack Kerouac and Neal Cassady visited Burroughs and his wife, Joan, here, a trip that Kerouac immortalized in *On the Road*.

In *Junkie,* Burroughs recalls the New Orleans he observed:

"New Orleans presents a stratified series of ruins. Along Bourbon Street are ruins of the 1920s. Down where the French Quarter blends into Skid Row are the ruins of an earlier stratum: chili joints, decaying hotels, old-time saloons with mahogany bars, spittoons, and crystal chandeliers. The ruins of 1900.

"There are people in New Orleans who have never been outside the city limits. The New Orleans accent is exactly similar to the accent of Brooklyn. The French Quarter is always crowded. Tourists, servicemen, merchant seamen, gamblers, perverts, drifters, and lamsters from every State in the Union. People wander around, unrelated, purposeless, most of them looking vaguely sullen and hostile. This is a place where you enjoy yourself. Even the criminals have come here to cool off and relax.

"But a complex pattern of tensions, like the electrical mazes devised by psychologists to unhinge the nervous systems of white rats and guinea pigs, keeps the unhappy pleasure-seekers in a condition of unconsummated alertness. For one thing, New Orleans is inordinately noisy. The drivers orient themselves largely by the use of their horns, like bats. The residents are surly. The transient population is completely miscellaneous and unrelated, so that you never know what sort of behavior to expect from anybody."

George Washington Cable (1844–1925)

Cable was born in New Orleans in 1844 in an old frame house on Annunciation Square. He was the fifth child of George Washington Cable and Rebecca Boardman, who moved to New Orleans from Indiana in 1837. He attended the Boys High School on Laurel St. near First St., but when his father died, George, still in his early teens, took over his job in the Custom House in order to help support the family.

After the fall of New Orleans to Union forces during the Civil War, the family moved to Mississippi rather than declare loyalty to the United States. Cable enlisted in the Confederate cavalry. After the South's defeat he ultimately returned to the city he loved. He married Louise Bartlett in 1869. They lived at 632 Dumaine in the French Quarter before settling in a lovely home at 1313 Eighth St. in the Garden District.

Cable began his writing career as an unsolicited contributor to

George Washington Cable

Historic New Orleans Collection. Acc. no. 1974.25.27.5

the *Picayune* in 1869. In 1870 he started a column called "Drop Shot" that appeared regularly for eighteen months and covered a wide range of subjects. In early 1871 he became a reporter, but he disliked the job and left the paper that year to be a cotton factor (an agent representing planters). He soon switched gears again, returned to the paper, and in 1873 met Edward King, a meeting that was to change his life. King had come to New Orleans with illustrator J. Wells Champney to work on a series of articles for *Scribner's* magazine called "The Great South." The two liked Cable so much that they agreed to further his career with publishers. As a result, Cable's story "'Sieur George" was published in the October

1873 issue of *Scribner's*. It was the beginning of a career that put stories set in New Orleans before a national readership and brought Cable friendships with some of the most powerful magazine editors of his time, among them Roswell Smith, Charles Scribner, and Richard Watson Gilder; the latter was instrumental in shaping Cable's work.

Today Cable is remembered primarily for his books *Old Creole Days* (1879) and *The Grandissimes* (1880), both of which were taken by "old" New Orleans society as critical treatments of the racial status quo as well as their mores and speech. The French-language newspaper *L'Abeille* ("the *Bee*") was consistently critical of Cable's writings, and Creole poet-priest Adrien Rouquette anonymously lampooned his work.

Cable was great friends with Lafcadio Hearn, and his national reputation brought him into contact with many of the great writers of his time—Mark Twain, Harriet Beecher Stowe, Charles Dudley Warner, Joel Chandler Harris, William Dean Howells, and Oscar Wilde, all of whom visited the house on Eighth St.

Cable's provocative stand on racial issues and his continued advocacy of the freedmen led to an attack by noted Louisiana historian Charles Gayarré and increasing social ostracism (illustrator Joseph Pennell once said that Cable was "the most cordially hated little man in New Orleans, and all on account of the Grandissimes"). Eventually, Cable and his family moved to Northampton, Massachusetts, where he was visited by such writers as J. M. Barrie and Arthur Conan Doyle, and where he wrote frequently about home culture and gardening—for example, in a charming little book entitled *The Amateur Garden*.

Cable was compared to Victor Hugo and Nathaniel Hawthorne; today his books are not widely read. He died in 1925.

Truman Capote (1924–1984)

Capote, a New Orleans native, was born Truman Streckfus Persons on September 30, 1924, at Touro Infirmary while his parents, Arch and Lillie Mae Persons, were visiting New Orleans and staying at the Monteleone Hotel. He lived in the Quarter at 711 Royal in 1945 while writing *Other Voices, Other Rooms*. He liked to socialize with the female impersonators at Gunga Den, a bar nearby. In George Plimpton's "oral biography" of Capote, this is how socialite Slim Keith described Capote's famous Black and White Ball, given November 28, 1966, at the Plaza Hotel in New York: "I think it was something a little boy from New Orleans had always dreamed of doing. He wanted to give the biggest and best goddamned party that anybody had ever heard of."

Maxine Cassin (1927–)

This native New Orleanian is the editor and publisher of New Orleans Poetry Journal Press Books. She lives in the Uptown area and is the author of four books, as well as the editor of numerous others.

John Chase (1905–1986)

An editorial cartoonist for the *New Orleans States,* Chase wrote the definitive and charming history of New Orleans street names, *Frenchmen, Desire, Good Children.* A New Orleans native, he studied at the Chicago Academy of Fine Arts and in 1924 went to work for Frank King, creator of the comic strip "Gasoline Alley." Chase came back to New Orleans in 1927 and began his career as an editorial cartoonist and writer. He is the coauthor of *New Orleans, Yesterday and Today* with four other writers. He lived at 4635 Music St. in Gentilly.

Kate Chopin (1851–1904)

Kate Chopin lived in New Orleans from 1870 to 1879. Her first child, son Jean Baptiste, was born here in 1871. Her husband, Oscar, was a cotton factor with offices in Union Street.

Early residences included the Chopins' first home at 443 Magazine St. (like the Pontelliers' residence in *The Awakening,* this was a double cottage shared with the family who lived next door at 445). By 1874 the family had moved to an Uptown residence at the corner of Constantinople and Pitt; it no longer exists. They moved to 1413 Louisiana, originally 229 Louisiana, in the "American" district, as the Garden District was called, in 1876. Chopin lived there until 1879.

Although most of Kate Chopin's life was spent outside Louisiana, her time from 1870 to 1884, first in New Orleans and then in the plantation country of Cloutierville and Natchitoches, marked her literary work forever. Two of her three novels and over half of her short stories are set in Louisiana. *The Awakening,* the best known of her books, is a classic reclaimed by scholars during the early days of the feminist movement. It depicts the life of Edna Pontellier, a married New Orleans society woman who longs for more than her life offers her.

"I don't mind walking," Edna says. "I always feel so sorry for women who don't like to walk; they miss so much—so many rare little glimpses of life; and we women learn so little of life on the whole." Chopin walked about the city a good bit, listening to stories, observing life on the streets, picking up the raw material that would inform her later work. Much of her time in New Orleans was consumed with the demands of a large family; long summers were spent in the coastal resort of Grand Isle, where Edna takes her fateful swim in *The Awakening.*

Marcus Bruce Christian (1900–1976)

Born in Mechanicsville (now Houma), Louisiana, Christian came to New Orleans when he was a teenager and set about establishing a dry cleaning business and a printing press. He was a contributing poet and reporter for the *Louisiana Weekly,* a black newspaper, when Lyle Saxon asked him to head a Negro unit of the Federal Writers Project in 1936. Christian's papers—more than a thousand poems, as well as research notes and unpublished manuscripts on the history of black Louisiana—are in the archives at the UNO Earl K. Long Library. Christian wrote *The Negro Ironworkers of Louisiana, 1718–1900.*

Winston Churchill (1871–1947)

Churchill, not to be confused with the British statesman, was an American historical novelist who lived in the Quarter at 613 Royal St. and 712 Royal St. He was the author of, among many other works, *The Celebrity* (1898), the best seller *Richard Carvel* (1899), and *The Great Crisis* (1901), a novel about the Civil War.

Andrei Codrescu (1946–)

Born in Transylvania, Codrescu has lived in the U.S. since 1966. He commutes to his teaching job at Louisiana State University in Baton Rouge. To the many listeners and fans of his work as a commentator for National Public Radio's *All Things Considered,* Codrescu is the voice of New Orleans. One of the city's most versatile writers, he is a poet, editor, essayist, and novelist. He is the author of more than twenty books, the most recent of which is the 1999 novel *Messiah.*

In his essay collection *Hail Babylon! In Search of the American City at the End of the Millennium,* Codrescu writes, "The nature of New Orleans is to encourage the optimum development of New Orleanians: it's an environment for a specific life form, a dreamy, lazy, sentimental, musical one, prey to hallucinations (not visions), tolerant, indolent, and gifted at storytelling. This goes against the very grain of American civilization as we know it."

Nicole Cooley (1967–)

Poet and novelist Nicole Cooley, daughter of Tulane faculty member and poet Peter Cooley, was born in Iowa and raised in New Orleans, where she attended the New Orleans Center for Creative Arts. She received the Walt Whitman Prize from the Academy of American Poets for her collection of poems *Resurrection.* Her first novel, *Judy Garland, Ginger Love,* was published in 1998. In an interview about that book, Cooley said, "I was afraid to write about New Orleans. Everyone had written about New Orleans and done a much better job. Every time I wrote about New Orleans it came out like a bad Tennessee Williams imitation. And then I thought, 'What about Airline Highway?' I thought about those motels and wondered what it would be like to live there." (Airline Highway, known for its seedy motels and run-down businesses, is an unlikely place for a young girl to grow up happily; it's also where the evangelist Jimmy Swaggart met his downfall.)

Peter Cooley (1941–)

Cooley, one of New Orleans's best-known poets, came to the city in 1975 to teach at Tulane, where he can number among his students such writers as children's author/illustrator Berthe Amoss, novelist Ellen Gilchrist, and poets Susan Prospere, Katherine Soniat, and Eric Tretheway. Cooley lives in suburban Jefferson, but New Orleans has been important to his work. In a 1992 interview upon the publication of his fifth collection of poems, he discussed the city's influence on him: "Although I haven't written about New Orleans in the way some other people have—by having obvious references to flora and fauna—it's changed the rhythm of my poetry, made it less tense and brittle and more pliant and relaxed. Now when I look back at my earlier work it seems black and white. It's important to me that other writers are here, writing. . . . And it matters to me that Tennessee Williams lived and worked here. It's a sense of context as much as contact."

John William Corrington (1932–1988)

Corrington grew up in Shreveport. He wrote novels, short stories, poetry, and screenplays and taught English at Loyola University and Louisiana State University from 1960 to 1933; he received a law degree in 1975 and briefly practiced. He was important in the circles of the *New Orleans Review* and the Loujon Press (and had a tempestuous friendship with Charles Bukowski). His best known works are the novel *And Wait for the Night,* the short-story collections *The Actes and Monuments* and *The Southern Reporter,* and his poetry, *Lines to the South and Other Poems.*

In the 1970s Corrington wrote scripts for such films as *The Omega Man, Box Car Bertha, Battle for the Planet of the Apes,* and *Killer Bees.* He and his wife, Joyce, also had a long and prosperous career as writers for the soap operas *Search for Tomorrow, Texas, General Hospital,* and *Capitol.* He was the writer and producer for the television series *Superior Court.* For a time, the Corringtons commuted between California and New Orleans but eventually settled out there. While in New Orleans, they lived at 1724 Valence St. Uptown.

Moira Crone (1952–)

Crone, a North Carolina native, is the author of *The Winnebago Mysteries, The Life of Lucy Fern,* and *A Period of Confinement.*

Her wonderful collection of short stories, *Dream State,* is set in Louisiana. She is married to the poet Rodger Kamenetz. The two live in Uptown New Orleans and commute to LSU in Baton Rouge, where both teach creative writing.

Tom Dent (1932–1998)

New Orleans native Tom Dent had a long and distinguished career as an activist and writer. He grew up on the campus of Dillard University, where his father was president, and he lived in Tremé during his later years. After his formal education at Morehouse, Syracuse University, and Goddard University and a stint in the army, he worked for the *New York Age,* a Harlem newspaper, and as press attaché for the NAACP Legal Defense Fund. In 1965 he came home to New Orleans. He was a founder of the Free Southern Theater, the author of the play *Ritual Murder,* about black-on-black crime, and the editor, with Richard Schechner and Gilbert Moses, of the 1969 book *The Free Southern Theater by the Free Southern Theater.* He wrote two volumes of poetry, *Magnolia Street* and *Blue Lights and River Songs,* as well as the 1996 memoir *Southern Journey: A Return to the Civil Rights Movement.*

Dorothy Dix (Elizabeth Meriwether Gilmer) (1861–1951)

Newspaper columnist Dorothy Dix—at one time a household name in America—was born Elizabeth Meriwether on a farm on the Kentucky-Tennessee border. She came to New Orleans in 1878 to work for the *Picayune* for the princely salary of $5 a week. Renting a room near the paper on Camp St., she set about learning her craft, doing the work she was assigned, reading newspapers from across the country and comparing their coverage of big stories, and memorizing editorials she liked. Her job on the *Picayune* was made possible through her friendship with the newspaper's publisher, Eliza Nicholson. Nicholson had befriended Gilmer in Bay St. Louis, Mississippi, where the young woman had gone to recover from strain and exhaustion after having discovered that the man she married, George Gilmer, was mentally unstable. Newspaper work seemed like a good way for her to support herself, and Nicholson was a formidable role model and mentor. For a time Gilmer lived at 1617 Jackson Ave.

In adopting the pseudonym Dorothy Dix, Gilmer perhaps patterned herself after her mentor, Nicholson, who wrote poetry as "Pearl Rivers." Gilmer wrote theater reviews, edited the women's page, and began an advice column that eventually was syndicated across the nation.

After sixteen years in New York covering murder trials for the *New York Journal,* Dix tired of the work. She returned to New Orleans in 1917 and lived in a house at 1225 General Pershing. During her later years, she served as president of Le Petit Salon and as a member of the board of directors of the *Times-Picayune.*

The gracious duplex facing Audubon Park at 6334 Prytania St. is where Dorothy Dix lived during the latter part of her life. She shared the house with her brother, Ed Meriwether, who lived downstairs with his family; she chose the upstairs quarters for her own. In 1936 *Time* magazine marked the fortieth anniversary of her newspaper column, which was published until 1949. Harnett Kane wrote an endearing, affectionate biography of her called *Dear Dorothy Dix.*

John Dos Passos (1896–1970)

The novelist lived at 510 Esplanade in February and March 1924, while he was finishing *Manhattan Transfer.* While in New Orleans, Dos Passos and newspaperman William McComb often visited a "regular Frankie and Johnny café called the Original Tripoli, full of vice . . . and rotten booze." His novel *Number One,* published in 1943, was a critique of demagoguery based on his fascination with Huey Long.

Tony Dunbar (1949–)

Mystery novelist Dunbar, known for his series featuring detective Tubby Dubonnet, a New Orleans attorney who enjoys the pleasures of the flesh, first came to New Orleans on a family vacation when he was fifteen years old. He recalls standing in the middle of Bourbon Street: "I'd never seen anything like it. And that experience planted the seeds of a desire to live in New Orleans." A graduate of Tulane Law School, he is also the author of three works of southern history, including the 1990 memoir *Delta Time,* in which he returned to the Mississippi landscape where he was a civil rights worker. He has lived in New Orleans since 1978. "New Orleans has given me a great place to live," he says. "And the lesson that the Delta has taught me is not to give up on the place you live." Now he fights the good fight in his detective fiction and in working for the group Eracism, which is committed to improving race relations.

Alice Dunbar-Nelson (1875–1935)

Born Alice Moore in New Orleans, Dunbar-Nelson grew up in a house at 56½ Palmyra in Carrollton and was educated at Straight College. She married the poet Paul Laurence Dunbar, then teacher Henry Callis, then journalist Robert John Nelson. She wrote poetry, fiction, drama, and journalism. Literary critic Gloria Hull focused critical attention on Dunbar-Nelson when she edited *Give Us Each Day: The Diary of Alice Dunbar-Nelson,* published in 1984, and Dunbar-Nelson's collected works, published in 1988.

Louis Edwards (1962–)

Edwards, a Lake Charles native, came to New Orleans in the fall of 1985 to do graduate work in English at the University of New Orleans. In January 1986 he went to work for the New Orleans Jazz and Heritage Festival. Now he divides his time between Festival Productions, which also produces the JVC Jazz Festival in New York, and writing fiction, most notably *Ten Seconds* and *N: A Romantic Mystery.* He is the recipient of a 1994 Whiting Writers Award and a 1993–94 Guggenheim Fellowship. His writing reflects the sadness arising out of black men's lives, a sadness he sees all around him in the city he loves.

When *N* came out in 1997, Edwards, in an interview in the *Times-Picayune,* said, "I just could not see another television news program about some black kid killing some other black kid for God knows what—we don't know what—and not do something. There's a lot of talk about what an artist should be and what sub-

William Spratling's drawing of himself and William Faulkner from
Sherwood Anderson and Other Famous Creoles

Historic New Orleans Collection. Acc. no. 73-320-6

ject matter should be. And I just thought I should take up the artistic challenge of trying to find out something about it, to document it, to somehow explore this real, real tragedy, that is a big part of our city, and the city's sadness at this moment."

William Faulkner (1897–1962)

When Faulkner first came to New Orleans in 1924, he was attracted here by the presence of the *Double Dealer* circle (the magazine had published his work in 1922) and of Sherwood Anderson, whose writing he very much admired. He stayed with the Andersons at their Pontalba Buildings apartment until he wore out his welcome, then moved in with artist William Spratling at 624 Pirate's Alley, overlooking St. Louis Cathedral's garden and now the home of Faulkner House Books. Faulkner wrote the text to accompany Spratling's drawings for *Sherwood Anderson and Other Famous Creoles,* which lampooned Quarter artistic circles.

While in New Orleans, Faulkner contributed sketches to the *Double Dealer* and the *Times-Picayune* and worked on *Soldier's Pay.* Two more of his works directly concern New Orleans: *Mosquitoes,* a satire of members of French Quarter artistic circles undertaking an outing on Lake Pontchartrain, and *Pylon,* inspired in part by the opening of Shushan Lakefront Airport on Ash Wednesday, 1934, and the tragic death of a young flyer during that event—a story that appealed to Faulkner's own love of flying.

Peter Feibleman (1930–)

New Orleans native Feibleman is the son of philosopher James K. Feibleman, who hobnobbed with Sherwood Anderson and other writers in the 1930s. Feibleman grew up in Metairie, but he was never far from the literary center of the period, even as a small child. He recalls the time his mother, Dorothy Broido, arrived to drive him home from dance class with Henry Miller passed out in the car. Once he went on a nature walk with William Faulkner that ended up at a liquor store. When he was ten, he met Lillian Hellman, with whom he lived near the end of her life. Today he is the executor of Hellman's estate.

Feibleman's first novel, *A Place without Twilight,* published in 1958, was written while he was an actor in Spain, and the young writer filled page after page with homesick memories of New Orleans. He is the author of three other novels—*Daughters of Necessity, The Columbus Tree,* and *Charlie Boy,* four novellas collected in *Strangers and Graves,* and five works of nonfiction—*The Bayou Country, The Cooking of Spain and Portugal, Creole and Acadian Cooking, Lilly: A Memoir,* and *Eating Together: Recollections and Recipes.*

Feibleman has returned to New Orleans on several occasions, for the New Orleans Writers Conference and the Tennessee Williams/New Orleans Literary Festival, as well as for the reissue by Louisiana State University Press, on the book's fortieth anniversary, of *A Place without Twilight*. "It's odd for me to go back to New Orleans," he said at a book-signing on that occasion. "It's not the New Orleans I knew, but then you get a whiff or a taste of it. I worry that no one will come to the bookstore. My father always used to say that New Orleans had produced more writers and fewer readers than any other city." (But on that February night in 1998, the Garden District Book Shop was packed.)

Edna Ferber (1887–1968)

One of the scenes in *Saratoga Trunk* took place at Madame Begue's Restaurant, now Tujague's, on Decatur St.

Eugene Field (1850–1895)

The poet and journalist lived at 628 Royal St. for a while, as well as Uptown in a boardinghouse at the corner of Fourth and Prytania.

F. Scott Fitzgerald (1896–1940)

Fitzgerald rented rooms—found with the help of Sherwood Anderson—at 2900 Prytania St. briefly in 1920 and seems not to have liked New Orleans much. He did, however, develop a liking for Sazeracs, the famous cocktails made at the Roosevelt Hotel; one biographer tells of the time he drove all the way to Montgomery with a pitcher of Sazeracs to see his beloved Zelda. The drink takes its name from a French cognac that, combined with the bitters invented by apothecary Antoine Peychaud, was originally sold as a remedy for stomachaches and other ills. The Sazerac Bar at the Fairmont is the place to sample one today. The recipe, from Kerri McCaffety's *Obituary Cocktail*, goes something like this:

one jigger cognac (rye whiskey is more commonly used)
crushed sugar cube
3 dashes Peychaud's bitters

2 dashes angostura bitters

Chill in shaker and strain into a glass laced with Pernod or Herbsaint. Garnish with a twist of lemon.

Richard Ford (1944–)

A native of Jackson, Mississippi, Ford has come to New Orleans off and on over the years to write, and he settled here for a while beginning in 1988, when his wife, Kristina, took a job as executive director of the City Planning Commission. New Orleans is mentioned, although only in passing, in several of his works. His novel *Independence Day* won a Pulitzer Prize and the PEN/Faulkner Award. *Rock Springs* is a collection of his short stories, and he edited *The Granta Book of the American Short Story*. In 1995, he received the Rea Award for the Short Story.

In a 1990 interview Ford said, "I'm not drawn to the mystique of New Orleans. I was a kid down here a lot. I've lived here off and on over the years in rented apartments. The external notion of New Orleans just doesn't feel right to me. I live in New Orleans as if it were just more or less another American city on a scale that I like. It's near where I grew up. My buddies come down here all the time. I've got friends close by. And I've got wonderful memories of places that I pass every day in the Quarter. But I don't want to spend my life trying to assimilate."

Patty Friedmann (1946–)

Friedmann, a New Orleans native, grew up here, went away to college at Smith, and settled here again in 1975. She is the author of *Too Smart to Be Rich: A Satiric Look at Being a Yuffie* (her term, short for "young urban failure") and two novels, *The Exact Image of Mother* and *Eleanor Rushing*. She lives in Carrollton. As to her continuing attraction to the city, she says, "Living in New Orleans is like working in the herpetarium. You know every day you're going to go home with a story that will make somebody shudder."

Charles Gayarré (1805–1895)

Gayarré, the foremost Creole intellectual of his era, lived in the cottage at 601 Bourbon St. (now a bar) in the late nineteenth

"There's one little place I'd like to show you after dinner," Johnny said. "Have you ever been to Chez When? I thought we'd have a drink there, and then I'm going to cash in too. You've got to watch yourself in New Orleans, Mac, or you'll be on the beach for a month."

"Blues in the night," hummed Bill, composing the tune as he went along. "I've got blues in the night. Okay, Johnny, one little drink and that's all. You don't think I mean it, Johnny, but I mean it."

They had a drink at Chez When. Then they had two at a place where there was a jazz band. Afterward they had one drink each in Pat O'Brien's, Dixie's and Cafe Lafitte. It was after one o'clock when they proceeded back up Bourbon Street.

"We kept it quiet, Billy boy," said Johnny proudly. "We kept it quiet."

—Robert Tallant, *Southern Territory*

century, but moved to a plantation in Mississippi after the loss of his family fortune during Reconstruction. Gayarré was Grace King's mentor as a historian and a bitter enemy of George Washington Cable. His four-volume history of Louisiana is still a major source of information; he was the third president of the Louisiana Historical Society, and his lectures and papers from twenty-eight years are collected in two of these volumes.

Carol Gelderman (1935–)

The Grosse Pointe, Michigan, native has lived in New Orleans for many years. She is the author of biographies of Henry Ford, Mary McCarthy, and Louis Auchincloss, as well as *All the President's Words: The Bully Pulpit and the Creation of the Virtual Presidency* (1997), an examination of presidential speechwriting and speechwriters. A self-described political junkie, Gelderman loves the Quarter but is temporarily in exile in the Garden District.

Ellen Gilchrist (1935–)

Mississippi native Gilchrist now divides her time between Ocean Springs, Mississippi, and Fayetteville, Arkansas. But just as with her critically acclaimed debut short story collection, *In the Land of Dreamy Dreams,* New Orleans still figures prominently in her work. Gilchrist moved to the city in 1968. She wrote articles for the *Vieux Carre Courier* and the literary magazine *Barataria* and established an abiding friendship with Rhoda Faust of the Maple Street Book Shop. The character Rhoda Manning, featured in much of Gilchrist's fiction, particularly the National Book Award–winning *Victory over Japan,* is named for Faust. Faust published Gilchrist's second book of poems, *Riding Out the Tropical Depression,* in 1986.

Gilchrist's New Orleans stories are rooted in perceptions of class difference and the tensions of modern life—the real world behind the land of dreamy dreams. Her female characters, determined to struggle for their freedom despite social constriction, strike a responsive chord with many readers. Long before Rebecca Wells's *Divine Secrets of the Ya-Ya Sisterhood* came along, Gilchrist's women were living outrageous lives.

Gilchrist's New Orleans landscape is also highly recognizable to local readers, whether it's the jogging track around Audubon Park where her characters work on their muscle tone, the buildings ate Tulane where they go to class, or the mansions on St. Charles Ave. and State St. where they live. "I think of myself as a New Orleans writer even if I'm not actually there," she said in a 1992 interview. Most New Orleanians think of her as a New Orleans writer too.

Shirley Ann Grau (1929–)

Grau shared a French Quarter apartment with her college room-mate, Mary Rohrberger, at 921 Chartres after leaving Newcomb, before her marriage to James K. Feibleman and move to old Metairie. Her first book was the collection *The Black Prince and Other Stories* (1955). Her 1964 novel of three generations of a southern dynasty, *The Keepers of the House,* won the 1965 Pulitzer Prize for fiction. Much of her other work is set in New Orleans, and she divides her time between the city and Martha's Vineyard.

John Howard Griffin (1920–1978)

Griffin began the odyssey that would become the book *Black Like Me* in New Orleans, November 1–14, 1959. He checked into the Monteleone Hotel and, with the help of an unnamed New Orleans dermatologist, began his transformation into a black man. He stayed, ironically enough, in the slave quarters of the St. Ann Street home of musician Harold Levy and his wife, then moved to a hotel on South Rampart, then to the YMCA on Dryades. Griffin talked with a Jackson Square shoeshine man, sought work unsuccessfully, and left the city for Mississippi. A significant portion of *Black Like Me* is devoted to his experience here.

Lee Meitzen Grue (1934–)

Grue, who lives in a beautiful home in Bywater, the neighborhood between Faubourg Marigny and the Mississippi, for many years hosted the meetings of the New Orleans Poetry Forum in a backyard theater. She edits the *New Laurel Review* and is the author of a short-story collection, *Goodbye, Silver, Silver Cloud* and a poetry collection, *In the Sweet Balance of the Flesh.*

November 1, 1959

Arrived by plane as night set in. I checked my bags at the Hotel Monteleone in the French Quarter and began walking.

Strange experience. When I was blind I came here and learned cane-walking in the French Quarter. Now, the most intense excitement filled me as I saw the places I visited while blind. I walked miles, trying to locate everything by sight that I once knew only by smell and sound. The streets were full of sightseers. I wandered among them, entranced by the narrow streets, the iron-grill balconies, the green plants and vines glimpsed in lighted flagstone courtyards. Every view was magical, whether it was a deserted, lamplit corner or the neon hubbub of Royal Street.

I walked past garish bars where hawkers urged me in to see "gorgeous girls" do their hip-shaking; and they left the doors open sufficiently to show dim, smoke-blue interiors crossed by long rays of pink spotlights that turned the seminude girls' flesh rose. I strolled on. Jazz blared from the bars. Odors of old stone and Creole cooking and coffee filled the streets.

At Broussard's, I had supper in a superb courtyard under the stars—*huîtres variées,* green salad, white wine and coffee; the same meal I had there in past years. I saw everything—the lanterns, the trees, the candlelit tables, the little fountain, as though I were looking through a fine camera lens. Surrounded by elegant waiters, elegant people and elegant food, I thought of the other parts of town where I would live in the days to come. Was there a place in New Orleans where a Negro could buy *huîtres variées?*

At ten I finished dinner and went to telephone an old friend who lives in New Orleans. He insisted I stay at his house, and I was relieved, for I foresaw all sorts of difficulties staying in a hotel while I turned into a Negro.

—John Howard Griffin, *Black Like Me*

Joel Chandler Harris (1848–1908)

The creator of Uncle Remus first ventured to New Orleans in October 1866, when, as a mere teenager, he came here to advance his literary ambitions through a position as the private secretary to William Evelyn, the editor of the magazine *Crescent Monthly*. Harris lived at the corner of Rampart and Canal Streets and spent an unhappy Christmas here; a story of his in *Uncle Remus's Home Magazine* in 1908 recalled the experience: "He was in a city far from home, and not at all happy in his new surroundings. He hung up his stocking, nevertheless, and woke to find it empty, and no wonder! Santa Claus could not have found him without a map of the town, and even then he would have needed a guide to show him the way to his small room in the top of a French boarding-house under the shadow of a great cathedral."

Evelyn was not disposed to publish much of the young man's work, and Harris soon went back to Georgia. After achieving great success with his Uncle Remus stories, he returned to New Orleans in May 1882 to discuss a proposed lecture tour with Mark Twain, who told him what a great success Harris's "Tar Baby" was when he, Twain, told it. While they were here, Harris and Twain attended church services with George Washington Cable, went to a cock-fight, and visited Cable's home, where waiting children were disappointed to find that "Uncle Remus" was white! Twain and Cable later went on a lecture tour together; Harris, it turned out, was too shy for such an enterprise.

Lafcadio Hearn (1850–1904)

Hearn originally came to Louisiana as the *Cincinnati Commercial*'s political correspondent. When he arrived here in 1878, the cheapest lodging he could find was in a rooming house at 228 Baronne St. He later lived with a Creole family at 39 Constance St., then with Mrs. Canterbury at 278 Canal St., then in a boardinghouse at 68 Gasquet (now Cleveland) St., run by Kate Higgins, and still later at 516 Bourbon St., opposite the Old French Opera House. He founded the Hard Times Restaurant in 1878 at 160 Dryades St. but lacked the temperament of a businessman; his partner ran away with all the money.

Hearn lived in New Orleans for ten years. He was the assistant editor of the *Item* as well as its first book critic, and later became the *Times-Democrat*'s first literary editor and translator. He contributed several articles to the official guidebook to the 1884 World Exposition. His published works include *"Gombo Zhebes": A Little Dictionary of Creole Proverbs* (1885); a cookbook, *La Cuisine Creole* (1885); and *Chita: A Memory of Last Island* (1889), a novel based on a real event, a hurricane that struck Louisiana's Ile Dernière in 1856, taking the lives of hundreds of vacationers and residents.

Hearn later emigrated to Japan and became famous for his writings about that country.

Lillian Hellman (1905–1984)

Max and Julia Hellman were living in the house at 1718 Prytania St. when Lillian was born in 1905. The boardinghouse was run by Hannah and Jenny Hellman, Max's sisters, who are the basis for characters in her play *Toys in the Attic*. The two women later moved to 1463 Prytania St., operating another boardinghouse there. Hellman's most evocative account of her young life is found in *An Unfinished Woman*, which recounts many of her New Orleans experiences; when she wrote of her childhood, she wrote mostly about New Orleans.

In 1910, when Lillian was five years old, her father moved the family to 1829 Valence St. The new home was a sign of Max's growing prosperity in the shoe-manufacturing business he had established in downtown New Orleans. The following year, however, the business failed and the family moved to New York, although Hellman would return, Persephone-like, to New Orleans for half of every year until she was sixteen.

Hellman last visited New Orleans in 1977, late in her life, when she spoke at Tulane along with her friend Peter Feibleman. At one remarkable moment she set her tissue on fire with the ash from her cigarette and seemed not to notice, although the audience was somewhat alarmed. Feibleman sprang to attention and quickly put it out.

William Kenneth Holditch (1933–)

Former Research Professor of English at UNO, Holditch is the acknowledged authority on New Orleans literature in general and Tennessee Williams and John Kennedy Toole in particular. Noted for conducting literary walking tours of the French Quarter clad in seersucker suit and straw hat, he remains a serious scholar, the editor of *In Old New Orleans*, a collection of essays about nineteenth-century New Orleans literature, and of the *Tennessee Williams Journal*. His essays, fiction, and reviews have appeared in many anthologies and journals. He and Mel Gussow are currently coediting Williams's plays for the Library of America.

Zora Neale Hurston (1903–1960)

Hurston stayed in Algiers while she was gathering material for *Mules and Men* in the 1930s, but she also visited the French Quarter.

Walter Isaacson (1952–)

A New Orleans native who grew up Uptown, Isaacson is the managing editor of *Time* magazine and a former reporter for the *States-Item*. He is the author of *Kissinger: A Biography* and *The Wise Men: Six Friends and The World They Made*, about the lives of statesmen Averell Harriman, Robert A. Lovett, Dean Acheson, Charles E. Bohlen, John J. McCloy, and George F. Kennan. "*The Wise Men* grew out of my fascination with old line establishment power (in New Orleans as well as in Washington)," he said in a 1992 interview. "I come from the sense that real power sometimes operates behind the scenes. Covering New Orleans and Louisiana politics is great training for any other political journalism. Nothing will ever seem more Byzantine than a Louisiana governor's race."

Brian Keith Jackson (1966–)

The New Orleans native moved to the Big Apple in 1990, where he launched a career as a playwright; he has had two plays produced by Theater for the New City, and his performance pieces have been presented at La Mama and the Soho Arts Festival. In 1997 he turned novelist with *The View from Here*, set in Mississippi in the 1930s, and followed that up with a second novel, *Walking through Mirrors*, set in contemporary Louisiana.

Rodger Kamenetz (1950–)

Kamenetz, a poet and scholar who lives in the Uptown university area, teaches creative writing and Jewish studies at LSU in Baton Rouge. He has written two books about his spiritual search: *The Jew in the Lotus,* the story of his meeting with the Dalai Lama, which was made into a 1998 documentary, and *Stalking Elijah: Adventures with Today's Jewish Mystical Masters.* His memoir *Terra Infirma* was published in 1998, and he is the author of two volumes of poetry.

Harnett Kane (1910–1984)

Kane was a newspaperman and historian whose best-known book is probably *Louisiana Hayride: The American Rehearsal for Dictatorship, 1928–1940.* He also wrote a biography of his colleague, *Dear Dorothy Dix,* as well as many other books. *Have Pen, Will Autograph* is a humorous account of the travails of the author tour, circa 1959. He lived at 5919 Freret, Uptown.

Richard Katrovas (1954–)

Poet Richard Katrovas has lived in New Orleans off and on since 1976; he has taught at UNO since 1983. "This is the first real home I've ever had," he said in a 1990 interview after his return from a Fulbright year in Yugoslavia. "Yet my relation to the city is such that I'll always feel like an outsider. I think that any adult who moves to New Orleans will always have that same feeling. In my work, I use the term 'resident tourist' to describe the way I feel about the city."

Jack Kerouac (1922–1969)

During Kerouac's famed visit to New Orleans, recounted in *On the Road,* he stayed with William S. Burroughs at 509 Wagner St. in Algiers.

Frances Parkinson Keyes (1885–1970)

The Beauregard-Keyes House, 1113 Chartres, is one of the French Quarter's most important landmarks and is open to the public for tours (there is an admission charge). It was built in 1826 for the grandfather of Paul Morphy, the chess champion, and was the residence of Confederate general P. G. T. Beauregard from 1866 to 1868. Keyes, who restored the house between 1944 and 1950, was a historical novelist perhaps best known for *Dinner at Antoine's,* published in 1948. She was also a famous hostess.

Grace King (1852–1932)

Grace King was the quintessential southern woman of letters. As mentioned earlier, her writing career began as the result of a challenge. When King voiced her disapproval of George Washington Cable's writing about the Creoles, Richard Watson Gilder, the editor of *Century* magazine, who was visiting New Orleans, asked her, "Why, if Cable is so false to you, do not some of you write better?" The very next day King began writing her first short story, "Monsieur Motte." Her literary work would expand to include some thirteen volumes of fiction and history.

As a friend and protégée of the great Louisiana historian Charles Gayarré (to whom she dedicated her 1895 work *New Orleans: The Place and the People*), King remained a conservative in her writing, much of which concerns New Orleans during the difficult period of Reconstruction, a time in which her own family suffered considerable losses. Although she ultimately revised her opinion of Cable's work, she remained a champion of the white southern cause all of her life. Her attitude in this regard once led to a falling-out with her old friend Gayarré when King suggested that stories of cruelty to blacks were better not published, lest they provide ammunition to proponents of racial equality.

King's home at 1749 Coliseum Street, on Coliseum Square, was the site of a famous literary salon where King played hostess to writers visiting New Orleans. She lived in the house with her brother and two sisters, and their attention to the details of daily life freed King to pursue her own interests and writing career. In addition to Gayarré, she numbered among her friends such luminaries as Mark Twain, whom she visited in Connecticut (and with whom she smoked cigars), Charles Dudley Warner, Julia Ward Howe, and Joaquin Miller. King's *Memories of a Southern Woman of Letters* is required reading for anyone wishing to understand New Orleans literary history.

Grace King as portrayed by artist Nell O'Brien ca. 1935
Historic New Orleans Collection. Acc. no. 1987.178.1

Yusef Komunyakaa (1947–)

Komunyakaa, the son of a Bogalusa, Louisiana, carpenter, won the 1994 Pulitzer Prize for poetry and the Tufts Poetry Award for his collection *Neon Vernacular.* When he lived in New Orleans in the mid-1980s, he taught elementary grades in the New Orleans public schools and English and poetry at UNO. He is currently a professor of English at Princeton University. His poems draw not only on his southern background and Louisiana childhood, but also on his experiences in the Vietnam War. His most recent work is *Thieves of Paradise* (1998).

Oliver La Farge (1901–1963)

La Farge came to New Orleans in early 1925 as an assistant in ethnology at what is now Tulane's Middle American Research Institute, an appointment that would last until July 1927. His French Quarter apartment at 714 St. Peter St. was known as the Wigwam

It is not that I became, or could become, an Orleanian. By descent I'm a pretty mixed sort of Yankee; at first in the presence of the Creoles I thought that I should jettison every aspect of Yankeedom, but I learned better than that. One cannot falsify his inheritance, one need not pretend not to be what one fundamentally is because he has added to it newfound goodnesses and ways of growth. I was not remade but educated, above all in certain simple things touching the happiness and wealth people can give each other. Of all that I have seen and done and felt in New Orleans in those early days and since then, the most important, the most significant summation I can give, is that I came there totally unknown and was thrown by chance among certain people. They were within me before I had time to mistrust them, and so for the first time I can remember I met them without any guard and put my heart in their hands freely. They never let me feel anything but gratitude that I did.

I opened my last novel, with the line, "New Orleans was a mystery and a promise," having in mind the French Quarter on a warm night. I condensed a lot of my feeling about the place into that line. Anything could happen there, in the blocks of houses too beautiful to be true, under balconies and in the shadows of the arches, and where the angling, jerry-built shacks have fought their way in among the ancient bricks. The hot nights stirred you until you had a cat's longing to prowl, down streets turned utterly silent, past speakeasies, by doors that gave out snatches of music, and the blocks where the whispers and eyes of the whores behind the shutters made a false promise of romance. Anything could happen in a town where the signs on the trolleys along Canal Street showed that one line ran to Desire and one to Elysian Fields.

—Oliver La Farge, *Raw Material*

and was a gathering place for artists, writers, and scientists. He was invited by the renowned archeologist Frans Blom to be assistant director of the first Tulane expedition to Central America. La Farge's first novel, *Laughing Boy,* was published in 1929 and received the Pulitzer Prize for literature in 1930. He left New Orleans in 1929, never to achieve such success again.

Clarence John Laughlin (1905–1985)

Writer and photographer Clarence John Laughlin, a Lake Charles native, is perhaps best known for *Ghosts along the Mississippi,* which through its depictions of the decaying remains of plantation culture chronicles a vanishing architecture and vanished way of life. A longtime Quarterite, he lived in the Pontalba Buildings. His work has recently been revived and celebrated in a collection of photographs and essays, *Haunter of Ruins: The Photography of Clarence John Laughlin.*

Nancy Lemann (1956–)

Lemann, daughter of a prominent New Orleans family, grew up Uptown. She is the author of four books, the best known of which is her first, *Lives of the Saints.* Her novels are dreamy, often hilarious evocations of New Orleans society. She now lives in San Diego.

Nicholas Lemann (1954–)

A New Orleans native and brother of Nancy Lemann, Nicholas Lemann is a serious social commentator in his books and journalism. In addition to being a former national correspondent for *Atlantic Monthly* and now a staff writer for the *New Yorker,* he is the author of *The Fast Track: Texans and Other Strivers; Out of the Forties; The Promised Land: The Great Black Migration and How It Changed America;* and *The Big Test: The Secret History of the American Meritocracy.* He lives in upstate New York.

Michael Lewis (1961–)

Lewis, the son of a prominent Uptown family, was a best-selling author before he was thirty, capturing the spirit of the 1980s in *Liar's Poker* (1989), about his experiences as an investment broker. He followed that with *The Money Culture, Pacific Rift,* and *Trail Fever,* the latter a diary of the 1996 presidential campaign.

In a 1997 interview, Lewis talked about the influence of New Orleans on him and two writer friends, fellow natives Nicholas Lemann and Walter Isaacson: "There's something about coming out of New Orleans that shaped us all. I write in response to a kind of irritation and to ease the pain in some way. It has to do with coming from a place where you've seen a way of life rapidly disappearing. Nick and I were talking—oh, maybe 10 or 15 years ago, and I asked him, 'Could you have gone back and lived your father's life?' [Lemann and Lewis are both sons of very successful attorneys.] He said, 'Oh, of course,' and I argued with him for a while and then we dropped it. But three years ago, he said, 'No chance, it's disappeared. . . .' So we have this sense of loss."

Malcolm Lowry (1909–1957)

The novelist and his wife stayed at a boardinghouse at 622 St. Ann in the Quarter in 1946. Lowry was finishing up the page proofs of *Under the Volcano,* which was published in 1947, and getting ready to journey to Haiti.

Everette Maddox (1945–1989)

A native of Montgomery, Alabama, Maddox came to New Orleans in 1975. He taught at Xavier University and the University of New Orleans. He founded the Sunday reading series at the Maple Leaf Bar and was coeditor of *The Maple Leaf Rag: An Anthology of New Orleans Poetry.* He published three collections of his poems, *The Everette Maddox Songbook, Bar Scotch,* and *American Waste.* Maddox called the Maple Leaf Bar "the only place where you can hear poetry, wash your clothes and get drunk at the same time."

William March (1893–1954)

"William March" was the pen name of novelist and short-story writer William Edward March Campbell, who lived in the French Quarter at 613 Dumaine St. from 1950 to 1954. March wrote *Company K* (1933), based on his Marine Corps experiences, and *The Bad Seed* (1954), about a murderous child. He came here after a nervous breakdown in New York and established a salon in the Quarter, where he achieved enough stability to enable him to complete the long-promised *Bad Seed* in the last year of his life.

Valerie Martin (1948–)

Martin, a Missouri native, grew up here and studied at UNO. She has taught there as well as Loyola University, Mt. Holyoke, the University of Alabama, and the University of Massachusetts. She is the author of two collections of short stories and five novels, the best-known of which, *Mary Reilly,* was made into a film starring Julia Roberts. Her most recent novel, *Italian Fever,* was published in 1999. She presently resides in Lagrangeville, New York.

Martin has lived all over the New Orleans, from Uptown to the Lakefront to Metairie to the 9th Ward. She says that it has given her "a sense of nature as both very seductive and very malignant. It's attractive and dangerous. And the city has given me an appreciation for corruption." She adds, "It doesn't change at all. It never changes."

Joaquin Miller (1837–1913)

Poet Joaquin Miller, born Cincinnatus Hiner Miller, was an Indiana native who came to New Orleans on a visit in 1884 to write about the Centennial Exposition for eastern newspapers. He stayed at George Washington Cable's home at 1313 Eighth St. while he was here and rode in a parade during the visit of Buffalo Bill's Wild West show.

Seth Morgan (1949–1990)

Morgan, the son of Frederick Morgan, the founder of the *Hudson Review,* came to New Orleans in 1986 to finish a novel he was then calling *Dead Man Walkin',* about his own experiences while serving prison time in Vacaville (California) for armed robbery. (Ironically, it would be published as *Homeboy,* while *Dead Man Walking* would later be the title of a best-selling work of nonfiction set in Louisiana, Sister Helen Prejean's account of her death row vigils.) Morgan came to New Orleans because, as he put it, he "ran out of highway." Through a housing program called Operation Comeback, he was able to purchase an old house in the Lower Garden District at 1232 Camp St. He tried to recover from drug and alcohol addictions while he was here, but the temptations of the city proved too much for him. He died in a motorcycle accident in 1990. At the time of his death, he was at work on a New Orleans–set novel called *Mambo Mephiste;* a fascinating excerpt from that unfinished novel was published in *Conjunctions 16* in 1991.

In an interview in 1990, Morgan said of New Orleans, "This is such a great town. It has an enormous fascination, almost a sexual allure, for me, like an aging courtesan. There's a kind of erotic morbidity, a sort of Latin confluence, but maybe I feel comfortable with that because I went to school in Mexico. There's not so much a promise of life but a guarantee of death.

"This is where I regained my sanity or a semblance of it. Ironically. This is such a honky-tonk burg. You can really stay messed up here in New Orleans very anonymously. But this is where I regained sobriety, sanity. The city's inherent tolerance, I know, was very helpful, and when it became necessary for me to reduce my life to utter simplicity, New Orleans was the place."

Vincent Nolte (1779–1856)

Nolte, a German-born merchant who wrote *Fifty Years in Both Hemispheres,* was the model for *Anthony Adverse* by Hervey Allen. He was also a friend of John James Audubon. His home at 710 Toulouse is known as the Court of the Two Lions for the figures that guard the courtyard, now a shop. This courtyard also appeared in Winston Churchill's novel *The Crossing.*

Eugene O'Neill (1888–1953)

The celebrated playwright is often alleged to have made his acting debut here at Le Petit Theatre, 616 St. Peter. In reality, he was here to join his touring father (the actor James O'Neill, famous for playing the title role in *The Count of Monte Cristo*). After a drunken rail journey to New Orleans, O'Neill took a part in a play and may have rehearsed it here, but he made his acting debut in Ogden, Utah.

The Court of Two Lions in a time when
the French Quarter was decidedly less touristy

Historic New Orleans Collection. Vieux Carré Survey Sq. 62.

Brenda Marie Osbey (1957–)

Osbey, a New Orleans native, has lived in the Tremé area and
explored its heritage in her writings. She is the author of four collections of poetry, one of which, *All Saints,* received the 1998
American Book Award.

"I'm a native native, I really am," she said in a 1998 interview.
"And that's important to me and to the work that I do. I don't want

my work to be mistaken for local color, but it often is. It's very easy for New Orleans to be thought of as a weird, odd, quirky kind of place. I'm writing against that stereotype, creating the New Orleans I know and almost never see in print."

Robert Palmer (1945–1997)

Palmer and his wife, writer JoBeth Briton, were living in a French Quarter apartment in 1995 when his final work, *Rock & Roll: An Unruly History,* a companion volume to a PBS series of the same name, was published. Palmer was the first rock and pop music critic for the *New York Times,* starting in 1976 and remaining to 1988. A gentle soul, he loved listening to New Orleans music, especially brass bands like the Soul Rebels.

In a 1995 interview, Palmer described taking Robert Plant and Jimmy Page to the Tremé Music Hall to hear the Soul Rebels. Plant was up on stage before the night was over and someone asked Palmer, "Was he in any band besides Led Zeppelin?" Palmer replied, with characteristic understatement, "I think Led Zeppelin was enough." He died in New York in 1997.

Walker Percy (1916–1990)

Bunt and Walker Percy moved to an Uptown house at 1450 Calhoun St. in September 1947, shortly after their marriage. Walker was receiving religious instruction from the Jesuits at Loyola University at the time, and his conversion to Catholicism distinguished and informed all of his fiction. The Percys lived here until 1948.

The Calhoun St. house has a serendipitous literary history. It was owned by Julius and Elise Friend. Julius had been an editor of the *Double Dealer,* which had published the work of William Alexander Percy, Percy's uncle, perhaps best known for his reminiscence *Lanterns on the Levee.*

From fall 1957 to fall 1959, Percy and his wife lived in an Uptown cottage at 1820 Milan part-time. They came here from nearby Covington in order to be close to their daughter's audiologist. The daughter, now Mary Percy Moores, was receiving frequent treatment at the time, and the long drive back and forth over Lake Pontchartrain was taking its toll on the Percys.

This neat one-story, two-bedroom house is a typical Louisiana home, with a small sunroom in the back. What happened here has captured the imagination of generations of readers: it is the place where Percy conceived of and began his National Book Award–winning novel *The Moviegoer,* published in 1961.

In a 1980 interview, "Why I Live Where I Live," for *Esquire* magazine, Percy said, "New Orleans may be too seductive for a writer. Known hereabouts as The Big Easy, it may be too easy, too pleasant. Faulkner was charmed to a standstill and didn't really get going until he returned to Mississippi and invented his county. The occupational hazard of the writer in New Orleans is a variety of the French flu, which might also be called Vieux Carre Syndrome. One is apt to turn fey, potter about a patio, and write feuilletons and vignettes or catty romans à clef, a pleasant enough life but for me too seductive.

"On the other hand, it is often a good idea to go against demographic trends, reverse the flight to the country, return to the ruined heart of the city. When the French Quarter is completely ruined by the tourists—and deserted by them—it will again be a good place to live. I'm sick of cutting grass. Covington lies at the green heart of green Louisiana, a green jungle of pines, azaleas, camellias, dogwood, grapevines, and billions of blades of grass. I've begun to hear the grass growing at night. It costs $25 to get my lawn mower fixed. If my wife would allow it, I would end my days in a French cottage on Rue Dauphine with a small patio and not a single blade of grass."

Tom Piazza (1955–)

Piazza is accomplished in many literary fields—he is the author of the short-story collection *Blues and Trouble* and several collections of music criticism, among them *The Guide to Classic Recorded Jazz* and *Blues Up and Down: Jazz in Our Time;* he also edited *Setting the Tempo.*

Piazza moved here in 1994 after graduating from the Iowa Writers Workshop. "I had loved New Orleans since I first visited here in 1987," he said in an interview. "And I didn't want to go back to

New York and I didn't want to stay in Iowa." He lives Uptown, which he loves, he says, "because of several things. The Maple Street Book Shop, for one. They are great friends to writers, and they've been very good to me. I like being close to the Tulane and Loyola libraries, and I like to be able to walk on the levee while I'm mulling things over. And there's a great snowball stand half a block from my house."

Katherine Anne Porter (1890–1980)

Porter was thirteen when her family moved to New Orleans and she remembers her education in the Ursuline convent. She liked to say that she "ran away from New Orleans and got married" at sixteen, but that may have been adapted from her aunt's history.

Porter came to live at 543 St. Ann in the Pontalba Buildings in September 1937, after falling in love with Albert Erskine, at the time the business manager of the *Southern Review.* She had met him the summer before at the Allen Tates' plantation home, Benfolly, in Clarksville, Tennessee. (She was nearly fifty; he was much younger.) Many of Porter's early short stories—"Old Mortality" and "Pale Horse, Pale Rider" among them—were published in the *Southern Review.* Robert Penn Warren and his wife took a room around the corner on Royal Street so they could come down from Baton Rouge and visit her for weekends. She and Erskine were married in New Orleans in 1938 with the Warrens as witnesses. The marriage was a disaster; the two separated in 1940.

William Sydney Porter (O. Henry) (1862–1910)

Fleeing embezzlement charges in Texas in 1896, Porter went into hiding somewhere on Bienville Street in a place called "the Rookery," or sometimes "the Ranch," where journalists hung out. He found work on the *New Orleans Delta* and the *Picayune.* New Orleans is the setting for four of his stories. In *Alias, O. Henry,* a biography by Gerald Langford, newspaperman Joe Monget reminisces, "The newspaper boys rented an old rookery down in the old French Quarter of New Orleans, where they slept and ate one meal per day—dinner. They called this place 'The Ranch.' They had employed one of the best Creole cooks to be obtained in the city, and I considered it a rare treat to be able to drop in to one of those dinners, both for the company and the food."

Sister Helen Prejean (1939–)

Sister Helen Prejean achieved national prominence with her 1993 best seller *Dead Man Walking,* later made into a film starring Susan Sarandon. Prejean grew up in Baton Rouge and entered her religious career in the Gentilly convent of St. Joseph Medaille. In 1980 she began working with people who lived in the St. Thomas Housing Project. Because many of the St. Thomas population had relatives in prison, Prejean became aware of the need for spiritual counseling for prisoners. She herself became a spiritual counselor to a death row inmate. Those experiences led to her subsequent activism against the death penalty and to her writing career.

Jean Redmann (1955–)

Redmann, who writes as J. M. Redmann, grew up in Ocean Springs, Mississippi, and moved to New Orleans in 1989. By day she is the counseling and testing coordinator for the NO/AIDS Task Force, and in her spare time she writes a mystery series featuring lesbian detective Micky Knight. One of these books, *Deaths of Jocasta,* was nominated for the prestigious Lambda Literary Award in 1992. Redmann lives in Marigny, "a funky old downtown neighborhood with great old Victorian houses."

Anne Rice (1941–)
Stan Rice (1942–)

The lovely, lilac Garden District mansion at 1237 First Street is home to New Orleans's best-known, best-selling writer, Anne Rice, a New Orleans native who has immortalized her hometown in the Vampire Chronicles, beginning with the phenomenal success of *Interview with the Vampire* (1976).

Rice, known for her impassioned novels of the supernatural, says that the house at First and Chestnut, called Rosegate, chose her. Haunted by the house itself, she used it as the setting of her best-selling saga *The Witching Hour,* about a family of Garden District witches and the male spirit, Lasher, who torments and tempts them across generations. Rice moved to the house in 1989; *The Witching Hour* was published in 1990.

Stan Rice, who was head of the creative writing department at San Francisco State University before he and Anne returned to New Orleans in 1988, is a poet. His *Singing Yet,* published in 1992, brought together new and earlier work. Stan is also a painter whose brilliant colors and primitive vision have won him a following in the local art world. A book featuring his art, *Paintings,* was published in 1997.

The First Street house was built in 1857 by Charles Pride, designed by James Calrow for Albert Hamilton Brevard, in a mixture of Greek Revival and Italianate styles. From 1947 to 1972 it was the home of the renowned federal judge John Minor Wisdom.

Another New Orleans residence associated with Anne Rice is 2524 St. Charles Ave., Uptown, where she lived when she was fourteen. The setting for her highly autobiographical novel *Violin,* it was owned by the Catholic church and had been a school, a convent, and a rectory before she purchased and restored it in 1995.

When the Rices first moved back to New Orleans in 1988, they lived at 1020 Philip St. in the Irish Channel. Anne Rice has said that she wanted to be near the place where she grew up, and this house is at the very heart of the landscape of her childhood. It is near Redemptorist School, and from her bedroom window she could see the steeples of the churches of St. Alphonsus and St. Mary's Assumption, important landmarks in her earlier life.

The other Uptown property associated with the Rice family is St. Elizabeth's Children's Home, 1314 Napoleon Ave. This complex was originally built in the 1830s as an orphanage for the Sisters of Charity of St. Vincent de Paul. The central part of the building was constructed as a school for girls in the 1860s and became an orphanage in 1870. The brick wings were added in the 1880s. Anne Rice does not live in the building—which occupies an entire city block—but it houses her famous doll collection. It is frequently open to the public for charity events and concerts and for autographings upon the publication of Rice's books.

Anne Rice speaks directly to her readers through a fan line, (504)

522-8634, and accepts their messages; her Web site is www.anne-rice.com.

Alan Rinehart

The noted book publisher once lived at 1022 Dumaine St. in the Quarter. His mother was the mystery writer Mary Roberts Rinehart; her portrait by Howard Chandler Christy hung on the second floor.

Adrien (1813–1887) and Dominique (1810–1890) Rouquette

The Rouquette brothers lived at 413 Royal St. in the French Quarter. Adrien was a poet and nature lover who became a missionary to the Choctaws. He is best known for *La Nouvelle Atala*. Dominique was also a poet. Look for the *R* in the ironwork on the balcony of the building, now the home of Moss Antiques.

Laura Joh Rowland (1953–)

Rowland, who came to New Orleans from Detroit in 1981, was for many years an engineer. In her spare time she created a series of mystery novels set in seventeenth-century Japan and featuring a samurai protagonist. They were so successful that she quit her engineering job in 1996. There are four volumes in the series—*Shinju, Bundori, The Way of the Traitor,* and *The Concubine's Tattoo.* Rowland lives in Gentilly. "New Orleans is a place that really nourishes the imagination," she says. "It's a city that loves artists and writers and other creative people. And the writers' community here has been really supportive."

Kalamu ya Salaam (1947–)

Born Vallery Ferdinand III, Salaam changed his name to the Swahili phrase for "pen of peace" in a 1970 Kwanzaa ceremony. A poet, dramatist, fiction writer, and music critic, Salaam is also the former executive director of the New Orleans Jazz and Heritage Festival, the former editor of *Black Collegian* magazine, and a former partner in Bright Moments, a public relations firm. One of his works-in-progress is *Black New Orleans: A Literary History.* "One of the things that has happened here is that we have not recognized our own greatness. New Orleans produced the first anthology of poetry by people of color, *Les Cenelles,* and it wasn't even in English," Salaam said in a 1994 interview.

"And Louis Armstrong's memoirs are great. And he wrote them. Here you have a musician who is literally one of the creators of the music we know as jazz, certainly one of the most known and admired musicians worldwide who has ever lived . . . who still found time and was inclined to write. Until his death, he wrote copious letters. And we're not talking about someone who went through ghostwriters. He actually owned a typewriter. I maintain that if his name had been Leo Stratacovich and he'd made that same kind of contribution, he would have been deified as a writer. . . . And then there's someone like Marcus Christian (poet, historian and teacher, director for 'The Colored Project,' the Federal Writers Project), who's done so much work yet is virtually unknown.

"Faulkner was not from here; Capote was not from here. They just came here and drank the nectar."

Salaam now lives in Algiers. "What I like about it is the river, We live six blocks from the river and I jog along the river in the morning. I've lived most of my life in Lower Ninth Ward, I spent a couple of years in the east, and I lived in that area, Parkchester, right off Paris Avenue for about two years, and I lived Uptown on General Pershing. Historically, coming up in the Lower Ninth really shaped me. It was the area I loved."

James Sallis (1944–)

Sallis, critic, poet, essayist and mystery novelist, first came to New Orleans in the mid- 1960s as a student at Tulane. In 1991 he returned to the city and rented an Uptown apartment on General Pershing. Sallis writes about New Orleans in his Lew Griffin mystery series, some five volumes—*The Long-Legged Fly, Moth, Black Hornet, Eye of the Cricket,* and *Bluebottle.* In a 1994 interview Sallis said of New Orleans, "It's a place of such extremes. I tend to like extremes. The edges are sharper here, the corners harder. There are so many levels here, culturally. You can go into any neighborhood and find all of New Orleans. . . . It's a city that takes itself seriously, but at the same time thinks of itself as party animal. It's a city with a tremendous history that's trying to destroy its history. I can get so irritated with the politics here, which anyone can, and I can get so upset about the racism here, which is really outrageous. But there is still a real attraction."

Sallis currently lives and writes in Arizona.

Lyle Saxon (1891–1946)

Lyle Saxon was one of the most beloved of all French Quarter residents. He was also one of the most important of all Louisiana writers, responsible for the production of the enduring WPA guides to New Orleans and to Louisiana.

Saxon came to New Orleans to write for various newspapers, spent a year in Chicago as a reporter, then returned to New Orleans in 1918 and eventually began writing for the *Times-Picayune*. He was a pioneer in his love for the old part of the city. When he first moved into the Quarter, his friends were horrified; it was a dangerous, rundown neighborhood. But he persevered, and others soon followed his lead. His first home in the Quarter was at 612 Royal Street; he rented sixteen rooms for the amazing sum of $16 a month. He loved these familiar old streets and wrote about them beautifully. He covered the fire that destroyed the French Opera House on December 4, 1919, sitting on a curb with artist friend Alberta Kinsey, watching the tragic destruction. "The heart of the old French Quarter has stopped beating," he wrote in the *Times-Picayune* in a story that is included in his book *Fabulous New Orleans*.

Other French Quarter addresses associated with Saxon include 536 Royal, a building he acquired in 1920 and lived in intermittently. He sold it in 1925 before moving to New York. He lived in an apartment at 627 St. Peter in early 1925 and moved into a third-floor apartment at 620 St. Peter in 1926. At the time, St. Peter St. was also the home of Roark Bradford, Oliver La Farge, and Samuel Louis Gilmore.

Perhaps Saxon's most famous French Quarter address was his final one. In 1937 he bought the house at 534 Madison St., still one of the loveliest French Quarter streets. The courtyard was a frequent setting for drinks prepared by Saxon's legendary manser-

Master mixologist Joe Gilmore (left) and writer Lyle Saxon
Historic New Orleans Collection. Acc. no. 1983.215.9

vant Joe Gilmore, celebrated as one of the best bartenders in town. Saxon began work on *The Friends of Joe Gilmore,* a loosely structured, hilarious autobiography that was also a tribute to his great friend, but died before completing it. Edward Dreyer, Saxon's long-time friend and collaborator on *Gumbo Ya-Ya* (the collection of Louisiana folklore published in 1945), finished the work by adding a section entitled "And Some Friends of Lyle Saxon."

Gwyn Conger and John Steinbeck were married in this house in March 1943. Saxon sold it the next year, repairing to his beloved St. Charles Hotel.

Fatima Shaik (1952–)
Shaik is a New Orleans native and the daughter of schoolteachers. Her first book was a collection of three novellas, *The Mayor*

of New Orleans: Just Talking Jazz (1987). Recently she has turned her attention to books for young readers and picture books for children. Her work has been anthologized many times, most recently in the 1997 *Men We Cherish: African-American Women Praise the Men in Their Lives*. She now lives in New York City, where she teaches at St. Peter's College, but she frequently returns to New Orleans to visit her family and to read from her work.

In an interview with Diane Simmons published in the *Xavier Review* in 1998, Shaik said, "I grew up in the 7th Ward. It's a black community, and it was a black community unlike a lot of the pictures of the black communities and the stereotypes. I'm really interested in writing for a mass market, and one of the reasons I am is because I find that so much that is marketable is stereotypical and negative and violent, and that's not the way I grew up at all.

"When I grew up it was magical, because my grandmother lived around the corner, my aunt lived down the block, and my mother taught in the school half a block away. There was an opera singer who lived on the corner and the fellow next door to us played jazz music. You couldn't have painted a nicer picture. I didn't even need to embellish [to create the portrait of a music-filled city in *The Mayor of New Orleans*] because that was my reality."

Robert Skinner (1948–)

Mystery novelist and scholar Robert Skinner came to New Orleans in 1979 to take a job with the Louisiana State University Medical School as a medical librarian. He has been the librarian at Xavier University since 1987 and the coeditor of the *Xavier Review* since 1989. The author of three novels set in the 1930s featuring detective Wesley Farrell, he is also a scholar of the work of Chester Himes (the African American detective novelist best known for *Cotton Comes to Harlem*) and has written about the hardboiled detective genre in *The Hardboiled Explicator* and *The New Hardboiled Dick: A Personal Checklist* (in a revised edition, *The New Hardboiled Dick: Heroes for a New Urban Mythology*).

Julie Smith (1944–)

Smith came here after college and worked at the *Times-Picayune* for a year. She is the author of two mystery series, one featuring

New Orleans homicide detective Skip Langdon. She received the Edgar Award for *New Orleans Mourning,* the first in the series, published in 1990. Her second series centers around Rebecca Schwartz, a San Francisco attorney.

Smith has lived in the French Quarter as well as Uptown. "In a lot of ways, New Orleans is the soul of my stories," she says. "It's a character as important as any of the human ones, and it's also an integral part of the soul of the human characters. Everywhere you turn, there it is, a kind of funky mortar, sticking the story together."

Henry Morton Stanley (1841–1904)

New Orleans was the boyhood home of adventurer Henry Morton Stanley, as in "Dr. Livingstone, I presume." Stanley was adopted by cotton merchant Henry Hope Stanley and his wife, who befriended him after young Henry, a runaway Welsh cabin boy, jumped ship. His house was originally located at 906 Orange St. but has been moved to 1729 Coliseum Square.

Robert Tallant (1909–1957)

Tallant was a native New Orleanian who became a folklorist. He worked under Lyle Saxon for Federal Writers Project in the 1940s and wrote *Voodoo in New Orleans* (1946), *Mardi Gras As It Was,* and the wonderfully comic Mrs. Candy novels, as well as many other books set in New Orleans, including the classic *Romantic New Orleanians.* He lived at 3324 Carondelet St. Uptown.

Edward Larocque Tinker (1881–1968)

Tinker, a New York lawyer, came to New Orleans as a result of his marriage to native Frances McKee Dodge. The couple lived in the Garden District at 1407 First St. Tinker developed a deep interest in Louisiana and became an authority on its history and lore. He wrote many books, including *Gombo: The Creole Dialect of Louisiana,* published in 1934, *Creole City* (1953), and *Old New Orleans,* a series of four novellas published in 1930 in collaboration with his wife.

John Kennedy Toole (1937–1969)

Toole lived in the upstairs front apartment at 390 Audubon St. Uptown. He found this place for his family when he was sixteen

Twilight was settling around the Night of Joy bar. Outside, Bourbon street was beginning to light up. Neon signs flashed off and on, reflecting in the streets dampened by the light mist that had been falling steadily for some time. The taxis bringing the evening's first customers, midwestern tourists and conventioneers, made slight splashing sounds in the cold dusk.

A few other customers were in the Night of Joy, a man who ran his finger along a racing form, a depressed blonde who seemed connected with the bar in some capacity, and an elegantly dressed young man who chainsmoked Salems and drank frozen daiquiris in gulps.

"Ignatius, we better go," Mrs. Reilly said and belched.

"What?" Ignatius bellowed. "We must stay to watch the corruption. It's already beginning to set in."

The elegant young man spilled his daiquiri on his bottle-green velvet jacket.

"Hey, bartender," Mrs. Reilly called. "Get a rag. One of the customers just spilled they drink."

"That's *quite* all right, darling," the young man said angrily. He arched an eyebrow at Ignatius and his mother. "I think I'm in the wrong bar anyway."

—John Kennedy Toole, *A Confederacy of Dunces*

and starting at Tulane, knowing that his parents would want to be close to the school and that they expected him to live at home. After graduating from Fortier High School, Toole wrote his first novel, *The Neon Bible,* published posthumously in 1990. He wrote *Confederacy of Dunces* while he was stationed in Puerto Rico during a tour of duty in the army. He was twenty-six years old when he completed the book, but he failed to find a publisher during his lifetime. He committed suicide in 1969.

For many, *Confederacy of Dunces* ranks as the best novel of contemporary New Orleans. The perambulations of Ignatius Reilly, sometime medievalist and purveyor of hot dogs, and his ensuing meditations are all written with a broad and wicked humor. The real sounds and smells and flavors of the streets of New Orleans are in this book, along with its many dialects.

In 1967, while teaching at Dominican, Toole moved to the cottage at 7632 Hampson Street, his final residence. After a pilgrimage to Flannery O'Connor's home in Georgia, Toole took his life in Biloxi, Mississippi.

Surely one of New Orleans's best-known and most tormented writers, Toole won the Pulitzer Prize in 1981, over a decade after his death. Ironically, Walker Percy's *Second Coming* was also nominated that year; Percy lost the prize to a book that he was largely responsible for bringing to publication. After Toole's death, his mother, Thelma Toole, pursued the older writer's attention doggedly. Finally he agreed to read the manuscript, was impressed, and encouraged Louisiana State University Press to publish the novel.

Mark Twain (Samuel Langhorne Clemens) (1835–1910)
Twain's life as a river pilot frequently brought him to New Orleans during the period 1857–1861, and he always insisted he got his pen name here. He didn't write about his experiences until *Life on the Mississippi* (1883).

Margaret Walker (1915–)
Walker, biographer of Richard Wright and author of the novel *Jubilee,* worked in New Orleans as part of the Federal Writers Pro-

ject. She spent much of her childhood in New Orleans and attended Gilbert Academy before going on to Northwestern University.

Jon Edgar Webb (1905?–1971) and Louise Webb

The Webbs, two of the most colorful characters to grace the New Orleans literary scene, first came here from the Midwest in the 1930s, migrated elsewhere, then settled here again from 1954 to 1967. In the 1960s Jon and Louise (universally known as Gypsy Lou) operated the Loujon Press at 638 Royal St. and 618 Ursulines in the French Quarter in the 1960s, publishing four beautiful books and one of the period's leading avant-garde magazines, the *Outsider*. They also lived at 1109 Royal St.

Jon Webb, a former newspaperman, was the author of a novel, *Four Steps to the Wall,* based on his prison experiences. (No one ever really understood how such a hardworking man with such high literary aspirations became involved with the armed robbery of a Cleveland jewelry store. He served three years in the Mansfield Reformatory, where he edited a prison newspaper.) Gypsy Lou sold her paintings at the corner of St. Peter and Royal by day, and helped Jon with the publishing venture at night.

The first issue of the *Outsider,* published in 1961, reads like a who's who of the beat generation, with work by Gary Snyder, Allen Ginsberg, Charles Olson, Edward Dorn, Henry Miller, LeRoi Jones, Colin Wilson, and William S. Burroughs. The first issue included eleven poems in "A Charles Bukowski Album," an indication of how strongly Webb was committed to Bukowski's work. Loujon Press published two of his books, *It Catches My Heart in Its Hands* in 1963 in two limited editions and *Crucifix in a Deathhand* in 1965, the latter in conjunction with New York publisher Lyle Stuart. The press also published Henry Miller's *Order and Chaos Chez Hans Reichel* and *Insomnia, or The Devil at Night.*

The Webbs moved to Tucson in 1967, seeking a healthier climate. The final two issues of the *Outsider* and the Henry Miller books were published there. Jon Webb died in 1971. Gypsy Lou lives in New Orleans today. "Where did we go?" she says of her life with Webb. "What did we do? Everything!"

Walt Whitman (1819–1892)

Whitman came to New Orleans in 1848; he and his brother lived at the Fremont Hotel across from the St. Charles Hotel. He wrote editorials for the *New Orleans Crescent* for a few months, then wrote occasional pieces for the *Picayune*. For a while he lived on Washington Avenue in the Garden District, but the building no longer exists. His "I Saw in Louisiana a Live Oak Growing," from *Leaves of Grass*, is one of the most famous poems associated with the state.

Thornton Wilder (1897–1975)

Wilder once rented a room in the house at 623 Bourbon, currently the residence of former congresswoman and United States ambassador to the Vatican Lindy Boggs.

Tennessee Williams (1911–1983)

Surely the most frequently asked question by tourists to the city is where they can see the fabled streetcar named Desire. For a long time they could visit it at the back of the French Market, where it was parked behind the Old U.S. Mint. No more. But the sound of a streetcar bell can still be heard each year at the Tennessee Williams/New Orleans Literary Festival when the former conductor of the Desire car rings one to announce the Stella and Stanley Shouting Contest, a springtime tradition.

No one has captured the heartbreak and romance of New Orleans better than Tennessee Williams, who often fled to the city to heal his personal wounds. It is also, as he told television interviewer Eric Paulsen, the place where he discovered "a certain flexibility in my sexual nature."

A number of French Quarter addresses are linked with America's most famous playwright. In the 1930s Williams lived at 620 Chartres and would go down the street to Victor's Restaurant at 601 Chartres and listen to the jukebox and drink (Victor's went out of business in the 1960s).

In 1939 Williams rented rooms at 722 Toulouse St., now a part of the Historic New Orleans Collection complex. He wrote the slogan for his landlady's restaurant (Meals for a Quarter in the Quarter)

Contemporaneous photograph of the house on St. Peter Street where
Tennessee Williams wrote *A Streetcar Named Desire*

Historic New Orleans Collection. Vieux Carré Survey Sq. 62

and occasionally helped out as a waiter. *Vieux Carre* is set in this building.

At 710 Orleans, in a second-floor apartment with a view of St. Anthony's Garden in the back of St. Louis Cathedral, Williams wrote *Ten Blocks on the Camino Real* in January 1946.

Most famously, 632 St. Peter, an 1842 townhouse that was once the home and studio of artist Achille Peretti, is where Tennessee Williams lived from October 1946 through March 1947 while writing *A Streetcar Named Desire*.

The playwright's final Quarter address was the house at 1014 Dumaine.

In a 1970 interview with New Orleans writer Don Lee Keith, Williams said, "In New Orleans, I found the kind of freedom I had always needed. And the shock of it against the puritanism of my nature has given me a subject, a theme, which I've probably never ceased exploiting."

Touring the French Quarter in 1971, Williams recalled his time here in a piece by Rex Reed for *Esquire* magazine: "This place has so many memories. I came here in 1939 to write. I was heartbroken over my sister Rose's confinement in a psychiatric hospital and I suffered a breakdown myself. In New Orleans I felt a freedom. I could catch my breath here. See that bar over there? That used to be called Victor's. I lived just around the corner in a large room on top of an old house where I worked under a skylight at a large refectory table writing *A Streetcar Named Desire*. At that time, I was under the impression that I was dying. I didn't feel much like eating, but in the evening after working all day my only close friend would bring me a bowl of oyster stew and in the afternoons I would go around the corner to Victor's Café and have myself two brandy alexanders. Without that sense of fatigue and that idea of imminently approaching death I doubt I could have created Blanche DuBois."

Observed Reed: "He talks as through Blanche is still inside him, trying to get out, a victim in the jungle without talons. His face is sad and old as he leads the way past antique shops, a flamenco parlor and a genuine voodoo shop, the owner of which claims to be a warlock who, in a former life, was a cat. The window is full of howling cats among the gris-gris, love potions and books on Marie Laveau the Voodoo Queen."

Christine Wiltz (1948–)

Wiltz, a New Orleans native, is the author of three mystery novels featuring Irish Channel detective Neal Rafferty, a novel of race relations called *Glass House,* and a biography of New Orleans's last celebrated madam, Norma Wallace, *The Last Madam: A Life in the New Orleans Underworld.* She also wrote and coproduced the TV documentary *Backlash: Race and the American Dream.*

In Wiltz's fiction, she has written about virtually every part of the city, from the French Quarter to the Garden District to the wilds of Westwego. "New Orleans is a rich and mysterious landscape of endless discovery," she said in a 1998 interview. "It's like a child's nesting egg toy, with an egg within an egg within an egg. You crack one only to find another." She lives in Uptown New Orleans.

Thomas Wolfe (1900–1938)

Wolfe visited New Orleans in 1937 and stayed at the Roosevelt Hotel, now the Fairmont. It was his first return to the South in seven years and a time of great crisis in his life, including the beginning of the end of his professional relationship with his influential editor, Maxwell Perkins, and with his publisher, Scribner's.

OTHER LITERARY LANDMARKS

Basement Book Shop

This sadly abandoned building at 7221 Zimple St. was once the center of literary life in Uptown New Orleans. It was home to the Basement Book Shop, so named because it was originally opened in the basement of a house in the 7700 block of St. Charles Ave. in 1928.

The bookshop was a gathering place for local writers largely because of the forceful personality and strong literary opinions of owner Tess Crager, and visiting writers from throughout the world made their way to the shop during its heyday. André Maurois appeared here during World War II to discuss the plight of his native France. Others who came were Edna St. Vincent Millay, Gertrude

Stein, W. H. Auden, Stephen Spender, T. H. White, and Alexander Woollcott (for whom Mrs. Crager made fudge). Crager and her husband, Robert, started a publishing company that produced the work of local literary luminaries, including Lyle Saxon, John Chase, and Robert Tallant. The company also published books about New Orleans cooking and gardening; one of its best sellers was the Brennan's Restaurant cookbook. The bookstore closed in 1981. Tess Crager died in 1985.

Buddy Bolden House

The famous jazz musician moved to 2309 First Street in Central City in 1887, when he was ten years old; he lived here until 1904. Built in 1871, the house is typical of the shotgun double style. Read Don Marquis's *In Search of Buddy Bolden* for factual information or Michael Ondaatje's novel *Coming through Slaughter* for a more impressionistic view of Bolden's life.

The Columns Hotel

Like the Napoleon House in the French Quarter, this hotel at 3811 St. Charles Avenue, right off the streetcar line, is a favorite haunt of writers and literati. It was the setting for the movie *Pretty Baby,* starring Brooke Shields. A late-night drink on its cool veranda, with the streetcars rumbling past, can be just the thing to induce inspiration—or relaxation.

Confederate Memorial Hall

Designed by architect Thomas Sully, this building at 929 Camp Street in the Central Business District is Louisiana's oldest museum, dedicated in 1891.

Degas House

The house at 2306 Esplanade in Esplanade Ridge was built for Michel Musson, the cotton dealer who was the French artist Edgar Degas's uncle. Degas visited the city from All Saints Day, 1872, through Mardi Gras 1873, during which time he painted *The Cotton Market, New Orleans*. The artist's stay here is recounted in Christopher Benfey's recent *Degas in New Orleans*.

The LeMonnier house, setting for
George Washington Cable's " 'Sieur George"

Historic New Orleans Collection. Vieux Carré Survey Sq. 42

The Double Dealer

The *Double Dealer* had offices at 201 Common Street and 203
Baronne St. in the Central Business District.

Hermann-Grima House

This French Quarter house/museum at 820 St. Louis may have
inspired Lermontant's home in Anne Rice's *Feast of All Saints*.

LeMonnier House

Famous as the setting for George Washington Cable's 1873 story " 'Sieur George," the LeMonnier House at 640 Royal St. is attributed to the architect Barthélémy Lafon; the LeMonnier (sometimes given as Lemonnier) family owned it until 1860.

Madame John's Legacy

This building at 632 Dumaine, French colonial in style although constructed under a Spanish regime, is one of the oldest in New Orleans, built in 1788 after a great fire that year destroyed most of the city. It was the setting for George Washington Cable's story " 'Tite Poulette," about a quadroon woman who received the house as a legacy of her white lover. If the West Indies–style gallery seems familiar, it's probably because part of the filming of Anne Rice's *Interview with the Vampire* took place here.

The Maple Leaf Bar

This down-home New Orleans landmark at 8316 Oak Street is the site of what has been called the South's longest-running poetry reading series, founded by poet Everette Maddox. Drop by any Sunday afternoon at three and see for yourself.

Monteleone Hotel

This historic Quarter hotel at 214 Royal St. boasts a long literary guest list. Truman Capote's parents were staying here when he was born in 1924. Over the years, the hotel has hosted William Faulkner, Richard Ford, Eudora Welty, and Tennessee Williams, who came with his grandfather.

The Napoleon House (Girod House)

Home of a popular French Quarter watering hole, the Napoleon House at 504 Chartres St., this building was built in 1814 for Nicholas Girod, mayor of New Orleans from 1812 to 1815. Girod planned to offer the house as a refuge to the defeated Napoleon Bonaparte.

Le Petit Salon

Originally known as the Victor David House, named for the hardware merchant for whom it was built in 1838, this building at 620 St. Peter St. next to Le Petit Theatre du Vieux Carre was purchased in 1925 by Le Petit Salon, a ladies' literary group founded by Grace King. The group restored the house; its members still meet there.

Old Ursuline Convent

This convent at 1112 Chartres St. is the oldest building in New Orleans, the only one to have survived from the period of French domination. It was begun in 1745 and is currently in use as an archdiocesan archive.

I would round the corner of the side street, move on toward St. Charles Avenue, and sit on a bench as if I were waiting for a streetcar until the boarders and the neighbors had gone to work or settled down for the post-breakfast rest that all Southern ladies thought necessary. Then I would run back to the fig tree, dodging in and out of bushes to make sure the house had no dangers for me. The fig tree was heavy, solid, comfortable, and I had, through time, convinced myself that it wanted me, missed me when I was absent, and approved all the rigging I had done for the happy days I spent in its arms: I had made a sling to hold the school books, a pulley rope for my lunch basket, a hole for the bottle of afternoon cream-soda pop, a fishing pole and a smelly little bag of elderly bait, a pillow embroidered with a picture of Henry Clay on a horse that I had stolen from Mrs. Stillman, one of my aunts' boarders, and a proper nail to hold my dress and shoes to keep them neat for the return to the house.

It was in the tree that I learned to read, filled with passions that can only come to the bookish, grasping, very young, bewildered by almost all of what I read, sweating in the attempt to understand a world of adults I fled from in real life, but desperately wanted to join in books. (I did not connect the grown men and women in literature with the grown men and women I saw around me. They were, to me, another species.)

—Lillian Hellman, *An Unfinished Woman*

A New Orleans Reading List

IF YOU'RE READING this book, you probably already have your own favorite New Orleans writers and books. Here are some of mine. Granted, some well-known authors associated with the city are missing from this list—Stephen Ambrose, Douglas Brinkley, Richard Ford, Carol Gelderman, and Laura Joh Rowland, for example, because although they are fine writers, their work is not directly related to the city or state. This is a highly idiosyncratic selection of personal favorites.

FICTION

Algren, Nelson. *A Walk on the Wild Side.* New York: Farrar Straus & Cudahy, 1956.

This novel of bohemian life in 1930s New Orleans is partly responsible for the city's reputation as a wild and wicked place. Thunder's Mouth Press reissued it in 1998 in a paperback reprint.

Austin, DorisJean, and Martin Simmons. *Streetlights: Illuminating Tales of the Black Urban Experience.* New York: Penguin, 1996.

This anthology includes stories by New Orleans writers Louis Edwards, Lolis Eric Elie, Kalamu ya Salaam, and Fatima Shaik.

Barnhardt, Wilton. *Gospel.* New York: St. Martin's Press, 1993.

Barnhardt, who is also the author of *Emma Who Saved My Life,* a remarkable debut novel about young people trying to make it in New York City, wrote *Gospel* while he was living in an apartment on Esplanade Ave. It is a long and complicated picaresque tale tracing the adventures of various individuals on the quest for a lost gospel, ending, appropriately enough, in an encounter with a Louisiana evangelist.

Barton, Fredrick. *With Extreme Prejudice.* New York: Villard Books, 1993.

Written by the film critic for *Gambit Weekly* and an English professor at the University of New Orleans, this is a thriller about a film critic trying to solve his wife's murder, with a punchy examination of prejudice in New Orleans and a healthy dollop of film criticism along the way.

Battle, Lois. *Storyville.* New York: Viking, 1993.

Inspired by E. J. Bellocq's photographs of Storyville prostitutes, Battle's novel is about the tangled lives of two women, a respectable Garden District lady and a Storyville madam, told during the height of fame of New Orleans's red light district.

Bennett, James Gordon. *My Father's Geisha.* New York: Delacorte, 1990.

The Moon Stops Here. New York: Doubleday, 1994.

Bennett's two novels recount the hilarious and heartbreaking saga of a dysfunctional but loving family, with a father away in the military, an alcoholic mother named Rosemary, a movie-struck daughter Cora, and a sadder but wiser young man named Teddy who worries incessantly about all of them. Bennett, a professor of English at LSU, often features Baton Rouge in his work.

Bonner, Thomas Jr., and Robert Skinner. *Above Ground: Stories of Life and Death by New Southern Writers.* New Orleans: Xavier Review Press, 1993.

This anthology of short fiction includes work by James Lee Burke, Fredrick Barton, James Colbert, Patty Friedmann, Martha Lacy Hall, and Joanna Leake.

Bosworth, Sheila. *Almost Innocent.* New York: Simon & Schuster, 1984.

Slow Poison. New York: Alfred A. Knopf, 1992.

Almost Innocent, told from the viewpoint of the young girl Clay-Lee Calvert, was an astonishing debut, a funny, wicked story of growing up Catholic. Bosworth's characters are often knowing young women who take in everything but are often undone by love.

Slow Poison, another novel of Catholic family life in New Orleans, features the Cade sisters, who are trying to come to terms with a complicated domestic situation that includes an alcoholic father. The "slow poison" of the title is both liquor and love.

Bradford, Roark. *How Come Christmas.* New York: Harper, 1948.
John Henry. New York: Harper, 1939.
Kingdom Coming. New York: Harper, 1933.
Let the Band Play Dixie. New York: Harper, 1934.
Ol' Man Adam an' His Chillun. New York: Harper, 1928.

Bradford, like many New Orleans writers, was fascinated by black folklore and culture, which he wrote about in his many books.

Bradley, John Ed. *The Best There Ever Was.* New York: Atlantic Monthly, 1990.
Love & Obits. New York: Atlantic Monthly, 1992.
Smoke. New York: Henry Holt, 1994.
Tupelo Nights. New York: Atlantic Monthly, 1988.

Bradley is an Opelousas, Louisiana, native who was a football star at LSU and later became a journalist at the *Washington Post* and a contributing editor for *Esquire* magazine. His novels draw on his life's experiences. *The Best There Ever Was* is a fictionalized version of the life of a famous LSU football coach, while *Love & Obits* describes the life of a Washington reporter. *Smoke,* Bradley's best work to date, draws on the author's small-town wisdom as two young men kidnap a fictionalized version of Sam Walton, blaming his giant discount stores for ruining their cherished way of life.

Brite, Poppy Z. *Drawing Blood.* New York: Delacorte, 1993.
Exquisite Corpse. New York: Simon & Schuster, 1996.
Lost Souls. New York: Delacorte, 1992.

Brite's horror novels are not for the fainthearted. In *Lost Souls,* she writes about vampires, in *Drawing Blood* about the violent world of an underground cartoonist, and in *Exquisite Corpse* about an unforgettable serial killer at work in the French Quarter.

Brown, John Gregory. *Decorations in a Ruined Cemetery.* Boston: Houghton Mifflin, 1994.
   The Wrecked, Blessed Body of Shelton Lafleur. Boston: Houghton Mifflin, 1996.
This native New Orleanian's first novel explores the tangled racial roots of an Irish Catholic family in New Orleans through the eyes of a young girl. In his second novel, Brown again explores race relations in New Orleans, this time through the eyes of an African American folk artist.

Burke, James Lee. *Black Cherry Blues.* Boston: Little, Brown, 1989.
   Burning Angel. New York: Hyperion, 1995.
   Cadillac Jukebox. New York: Hyperion, 1996.
   Dixie City Jam. New York: Hyperion, 1994.
   Heaven's Prisoners. New York: Henry Holt, 1988.
   In the Electric Mist with Confederate Dead. New York: Hyperion, 1993.
   Morning for Flamingoes. Boston: Little, Brown, 1990.
   Neon Rain. New York: Henry Holt, 1986.
   A Stained White Radiance. New York: Hyperion, 1992.
   Sunset Limited. New York: Doubleday, 1998.
Burke, a Louisiana native, is the author of many novels and stories set elsewhere, but he has achieved his greatest success with the detective series featuring Dave Robicheaux, a recovering alcoholic and former New Orleans police officer who is now based in New Iberia but whose life and work frequently bring him back to the city. The struggle for Dave's soul—will the violence around him become part of him? will he start drinking again?—that is at the heart of each of these novels keeps readers tuning in for new installments. But more than that, Burke manages to portray an increasingly violent world in a style that possesses a kind of shocking poetry, demonstrating time and time again the legacy of violence that is

central to American—and Louisiana—history. No one evokes the south Louisiana landscape, in all its threatening beauty, the way Burke does.

Butler, Robert Olen. *A Good Scent from a Strange Mountain.* New York, Henry Holt, 1992.

This collection of short stories won the Pulitzer Prize for fiction in 1993. Butler, who served in Vietnam, became proficient in the Vietnamese language and fell in love with the Vietnamese people, a love that shines through in these delicate, romantic, often humorous stories of cultural difference. Many of these stories are set in a real-life Vietnamese enclave called Versailles in east New Orleans. The lives of Vietnamese immigrants in a strange land, struggling between the old and the new, are treated with dignity, gentle humor, and compassion. Butler is also the author of six previous works, all recently reissued in paperback: *Alleys of Eden, Countrymen of Bones, Deuce, On Distant Ground, Sun Dogs,* and *Wabash.* He followed *Good Scent* with a controversial erotic novel called *They Whisper.*

Tabloid Dreams. New York: Henry Holt, 1996.

These stories have titles that come straight out of the tabloid headlines—"Boy Born with Tattoo of Elvis," "Help Me Find My Spaceman Lover," or "Titanic Survivor Speaks through Waterbed." Butler skillfully takes the reader into the human drama and comedy underlying each one.

The Deep Green Sea. New York: Henry Holt, 1998.

This novel, rooted in Vietnamese mythology, is the story of a Vietnam veteran, Benjamin Cole, who returns to that country in search of personal peace, only to become involved in a tragic romance with a tour guide named Tien. This highly erotic work is graced with the language of fairy tale and fable.

Cable, George Washington. *The Grandissimes.* New York: Scribner's, 1880; revised 1883.

Old Creole Days. New York: Scribner's, 1879.

Strange True Stories of Louisiana. New York: Scribner's, 1889.

Cable criticized the racism in Creole society, criticism that even-

Robert Olen Butler on familiar ground

Courtesy New Orleans Times-Picayune, *photo by Norman Berteaux*

tually made him quite unpopular in New Orleans society. Several of his short stories, most notably " 'Tite Poulette" and " 'Sieur George," are associated with the French Quarter's historic buildings.

Capote, Truman. *A Christmas Memory.* Available in many editions.
Music for Chameleons. New York: Random House, 1980.
One Christmas. New York: Random House, 1983.
Other Voices, Other Rooms. New York: Random House, 1948.
Of course, Capote's masterpiece, *In Cold Blood* (1966), told a true story of murder in Kansas. But Capote employed a Louisiana plantation as the setting for *Other Voices, Other Rooms,* and *One Christmas* is set in New Orleans. One of his most memorable short stories, "Dazzle," is about an eight-year-old Garden District boy who confesses his longing to be a girl.

Chopin, Kate. *The Awakening*. Chicago, H.S. Stone, 1899.

Finally recognized as an American classic, Chopin's best-known novel is a story of a woman coming to terms with her desires.

The Complete Works of Kate Chopin. Edited by Per Seyersted. Baton Rouge: Louisiana State University Press, 1969.

Codrescu, Andrei. *Messiah*. New York: Simon & Schuster, 1999.

Leave it to Codrescu to imagine a millennial Mardi Gras combined with the Apocalypse. Dante is a policeman, Karl Marx is working for the Sewerage and Water Board, and Nostradamus is a waiter at the Napoleon House. And it all somehow works out.

Cooley, Nicole. *Judy Garland, Ginger Love*. New York: Regan-Books, 1998.

Cooley, an award-winning poet, has written a harrowing first novel about a family of women who choose Judy Garland's life as the basis for family mythology. Central to the novel's theme is the image of two little girls sitting in a swimming pool on Airline Highway playing with paper dolls.

Corrington, John William. *The Collected Stories of John William Corrington*. Columbia: University of Missouri Press, 1989.

Corrington, John William, and Joyce Corrington. *A Civil Death*. New York: Viking/Penguin, 1987.

A Project Named Desire. New York: Viking Penguin, 1987.

So Small a Carnival. New York: Viking/Penguin, 1986.

The White Zone. New York: Viking/Penguin, 1987.

Corrington's collected stories were published posthumously. The detective series he coauthored with his wife, Joyce, featuring a black detective named Rat Trap, is out of print but well worth looking for.

Crais, Robert. *Voodoo River*. New York: Hyperion, 1995.

Crais, a Louisiana native, is a television writer who's also had great success with his series featuring private detective Elvis Cole and his remarkable sidekick Joe Pike. This novel brings Elvis to Louisiana.

Crone, Moira. *Dream State.* Jackson: University Press of Mississippi, 1995.

Crone taps into the otherworldly quality of Louisiana with these
wonderful stories, many set in New Orleans. Most have female pro-
tagonists who capture the dreamy dilemmas of life in Louisiana,
the lassitude and charm of the atmosphere.

Daniell, Rosemary. *Hurricane Season.* New York: William Morrow, 1992.

This graphic, often shocking novel, with settings in Metairie as
well as the French Quarter, is about Easter O'Brian, a woman artist
struggling to find happiness and fulfillment despite a tangle of violent, disturbed family relationships. Daniell is also the author of
the wonderful memoir *Fatal Flowers: Sin, Sex, and Suicide in the
Deep South,* as well as a book about writing titled *The Woman
Who Spilled Words All over Herself.*

Davis, Albert Belisle. *Leechtime.* Baton Rouge: Louisiana State University Press, 1989.

Marquis at Bay. Baton Rouge: Louisiana State University Press,
1992.

Davis, who teaches English and creative writing at Nicholls State
University in Thibodaux, is at work on the third novel of the projected "Mondebon" trilogy, which deals with life on the bayou and
in New Orleans and with the tangled legacies of family responsi-
bility, race, and culture.

Dos Passos, John. *The Forty-second Parallel.* New York: Harcourt,
1937.

A volume in the *USA* trilogy. Dos Passos also worked on *Manhattan Transfer* while living here.

Dubus, Andre. *Selected Stories.* Boston: David R. Godine, 1988.

Dubus, a Louisiana native who lived and wrote largely in Massachusetts, received both a MacArthur "genius" grant and the Rea
Award for the Short Story. Only a few of his works are set in Louisiana, but every story is a gem.

Dunbar, Tony. *City of Beads*. New York: G.P. Putnam's Sons, 1995.
The Crime Czar. New York, Dell, 1998.
Crooked Man. New York: G. P. Putnam's Sons, 1994.
Shelter from the Storm. New York: G. P. Putnam's Sons, 1998.
Trick Question. New York: G. P. Putnam's Sons, 1996.
Dunbar, a New Orleans attorney, writes about New Orleans attorney Tubby Dubonnet, who always seems to end up in the weird kind of trouble that only New Orleans can offer. *Shelter from the Storm* is one of the funniest Mardi Gras novels ever—and Tubby Dubonnet wins the contest for best-fed New Orleans detective hands down.

Edwards, Louis. *N: A Romantic Mystery*. New York: Dutton, 1997.
Ten Seconds. St. Paul, Minn.: Graywolf, 1991.
Edwards, a Lake Charles native who now lives in New Orleans, made a fine debut with *Ten Seconds,* a compressed story of one young African American man's life. *N* is rooted in the noir tradition in film and literature and describes a young African American journalist's attempt to get at the truth about the deaths of young black men in New Orleans.

Faulkner, William. *Absalom, Absalom!* Available in many editions.
Mosquitoes. Available in many editions.
New Orleans Sketches. Edited and with an introduction by Carvel Collins. Rutgers University Press, 1958.
Pylon. Available in many editions.
The Wild Palms. Available in many editions.

Feibleman, Peter. *A Place without Twilight*. Baton Rouge: Louisiana State University Press Voices of the South series, 1997 paperback.
A reissue of a 1958 novel by the New Orleans native, also known for *Lilly,* his book of reminiscences about Lillian Hellman.

Fennelly, Tony. *The Closet Hanging*. New York: Carroll & Graf, 1987.
The Glory Hole Murders. New York: Carroll & Graf, 1985.
Fennelly's outrageous mystery series traces the adventures of

Matt Sinclair, gay antique dealer and sleuth. Not for the faint of heart or rigid of outlook. Unfortunately now out of print.

The Hippie in the Wall. New York: St. Martin's, 1994.

1-900-DEAD. New York: St. Martin's, 1996.

This is a new series featuring a *Times-Picayune* gossip columnist named Margo Fortier as the detective.

Friedmann, Patty. *The Exact Image of Mother.* New York: Viking, 1991.

Friedmann, a humorist who is also the author of *Too Smart to Be Rich* and coiner of the term "Young Urban Failure," here writes about growing up Jewish in New Orleans. Her writing is filled with black humor and a wicked edge.

Eleanor Rushing. Washington, D.C.: Counterpoint, 1999.

This novel, set in contemporary New Orleans, is a first-person narrative of a young woman's erotic obsessions.

Gaines, Ernest J. *The Autobiography of Miss Jane Pittman.* New York: Dial, 1971.

Catherine Carmier. New York: Atheneum, 1964.

A Gathering of Old Men. New York: Alfred A. Knopf, 1983.

In My Father's House. New York: Alfred A. Knopf, 1978.

A Lesson before Dying. New York: Alfred A. Knopf, 1993.

Of Love and Dust. New York: Dial Press, 1967.

Gaines, born in the former slave quarters of a plantation near New Roads, Louisiana, has written movingly of African Americans claiming their identity. *The Autobiography of Miss Jane Pittman,* the story of a woman's triumph over slavery, is taught as a classic of African American literature. It is known worldwide, largely because of the film starring Cecily Tyson in the title role. Gaines's most recent book, *A Lesson before Dying,* is a tale of a schoolteacher in a small Louisiana town who takes on a difficult death-row pupil in order to teach him how to be a man before he faces death. It was chosen as an Oprah Book Club selection and received the National Book Critics Circle Award for Fiction, and was made into a movie for HBO in 1999. (*A Gathering of Old Men* was also made into a television movie.) Gaines is also the recipient of a MacArthur "genius" grant. His books, rooted in the rural Louisiana of his child-hood, are profound lessons in the heroism to be found in the lives of ordinary men.

Gautreaux, Tim. *The Next Step in the Dance*. New York: Picador, 1998.
Same Place, Same Things. New York: St. Martin's, 1996.
Welding with Children. New York: Picador, 1999.
Gautreaux is a rising star in Louisiana fiction who teaches at Southeastern Louisiana University in Hammond. His critically ac-claimed short story collection *Same Place, Same Things* captures the essence of small-town Louisiana in a loving, realistic, and often humorous way. Gautreaux's first novel, *The Next Step in the Dance,* chronicles the fortunes of Paul Thibodeaux and Colette Jeansomme, who grew up together in the fictional small town of Tiger Island, Louisiana. Devastated by the ups and downs of their marriage, as well as the economic setbacks and social change brought about by the 1980s oil bust, the two separate but meet in California, where they are seeking a better life. Eventually they wind up back in Tiger Island, struggling to make a living and to find their way back to each other. Gautreaux's second short-story collection, *Welding with Children,* continues his exploration of fam-ily life and community in Cajun country.

Gilchrist, Ellen. *The Age of Miracles*. Boston: Little, Brown, 1995.
The Anna Papers. Boston: Little, Brown, 1988.
The Annunciation. Boston: Little, Brown, 1983.
The Courts of Love. Boston: Little, Brown, 1996.
Drunk with Love. Boston: Little, Brown, 1986.
Falling through Space: The Journals of Ellen Gilchrist. Boston: Little, Brown, 1987.
Flights of Angels. New York: Little, Brown, 1998.
I Cannot Get You Close Enough. Boston: Little, Brown, 1990.
In the Land of Dreamy Dreams. Fayetteville: University of Arkansas Press, 1981.
Light Can Be Both Wave and Particle. Boston: Little, Brown, 1989.
Net of Jewels. Boston: Little, Brown, 1992.

Rhoda: A Life in Stories. Boston: Little, Brown, 1995.

Sarah Conley: A Novel. Boston: Little, Brown, 1997.

Starcarbon: A Meditation on Love. Boston: Little, Brown, 1994.

Victory over Japan. Boston: Little, Brown, 1984.

With a few exceptions, Gilchrist's novels and stories feature recurring characters, strong women facing problems of life and love, irrepressible and outrageous and free. *Victory over Japan* won a National Book Award.

Grau, Shirley Ann. *The Black Prince and Other Stories.* New York: Knopf, 1955.

The House on Coliseum Street. New York, Knopf, 1961.

The Keepers of the House. New York: Knopf, 1964.

Nine Women. New York: Knopf, 1985.

Roadwalkers. New York: Alfred A. Knopf, 1994.

Grau's short stories and novels often treat the grand southern themes of race and family. She won the 1965 Pulitzer Prize for *The Keepers of the House.*

Grue, Lee Meitzen. *Goodbye, Silver, Silver Cloud: New Orleans Stories.* Austin: Plain View Press, 1994.

Grue, a popular New Orleans poet and the editor of the *New Laurel Review,* displays a poet's sensibility in these fanciful stories, many set in the French Quarter.

Hambly, Barbara. *Fever Season.* New York: Bantam, 1998.

A Free Man of Color. New York: Bantam, 1997.

Graveyard Dust. New York: Bantam, 1999.

Hambly's well-written historical novels feature the exploits of Benjamin January, physician, music teacher, and free man of color in old New Orleans.

Henry, O. (W. S. Porter). *The Collected Stories of O. Henry.* Available in many editions.

"Blind Man's Holiday," "Cherchez la Femme," "Renaissance at Charleroi," and "Whistling Dick's Christmas Stocking" are the O. Henry stories with New Orleans settings.

Keyes, Frances Parkinson. *Crescent Carnival.* New York: Messner, 1942.

Dinner at Antoine's. New York: Messner, 1948.

These are only two of the best known of Keyes's historical romances. They are period pieces; enjoy them for what they are. They are readily available in the city's secondhand bookstores. Keyes is also the author of *All This Is Louisiana,* a state history with wonderful photographs, and wrote religious biographies, a cookbook, and a charming autobiographical work, *Cost of a Best-Seller.*

King, Grace. *Balcony Stories.* 1893; reprint New York: Garrett Press, 1969.

Monsieur Motte. New York: A. C. Armstrong and Son, 1888.

New Orleans: The Place and the People. New York: Macmillan, 1895.

Tales of a Time and Place. 1892; reprint: New York: Garrett Press, 1969.

If you can track down a copy of King's out of print *Memories of a Southern Woman of Letters,* you will gain a new appreciation for this formidable woman's achievements.

Lemann, Nancy. *The Fiery Pantheon.* New York: Scribner's, 1998.

Lives of the Saints. New York: Knopf, 1985.

The Ritz of the Bayou. New York: Knopf, 1987.

Sportsman's Paradise. New York: Knopf, 1992.

Lemann writes dreamy, almost incantatory novels of southern women falling in and out of love. *The Ritz of the Bayou* is a non-fiction work about the first corruption trial of former Louisiana governor Edwin Edwards.

Martin, Valerie. *Alexandra.* New York: Farrar, Straus & Giroux, 1979.

The Consolation of Nature and Other Stories. Boston: Houghton Mifflin, 1988.

The Great Divorce. Garden City, N.Y.: Doubleday, 1994.

Love. Amherst: Lynx House, 1976.

Mary Reilly. Garden City, N.Y.: Doubleday, 1990.

A Recent Martyr. Boston: Houghton Mifflin, 1987.

Set in Motion. New York: Farrar, Straus & Giroux, 1978.

Martin's best-known work is *Mary Reilly,* a historical novel in which Dr. Jekyll's housemaid is the main character; it was made into a movie starring Julia Roberts in the title role. Martin's other books, set primarily in contemporary times, are edgy tales of sex and power and violence. In *The Great Divorce,* my favorite of her works, she reinvents the idea of cat people in a tale of women and great cats in both historical and contemporary settings. The "great divorce" of the title is between man and nature, an enduring theme in Martin's work.

Miller, John, and Genevieve Anderson, eds. *New Orleans Stories.* San Francisco: Chronicle Books, 1992.

This is a wonderful anthology, with selections ranging from Anne Rice to Mark Twain, John Kennedy Toole, and William Makepeace Thackeray, and an introduction by Andrei Codrescu. A great introduction to the writings associated with the city.

Neihart, Ben. *Hey, Joe!* New York: Simon & Schuster, 1996.

This debut novel—sweet and sad and moving—describes the life of a young teenager, a student at a private school who is struggling to come to terms with his gay identity.

Nero, Clarence. *Cheekie: A Child out of the Desire.* Tulsa: Council Oak Books, 1998.

Nero, who grew up in the notorious Desire housing project, made his fictional debut with this autobiographical tale of an insouciant young boy coming of age in the 1970s. It has been published as a book for young readers, but some graphic sex scenes and language make it more suitable for adults.

Ondaatje, Michael. *Coming through Slaughter.* New York: W. W. Norton, 1976.

This impressionistic, lyrical novel centers around the life of the famous musician Buddy Bolden. Ondaatje is probably better known for his best-seller *The English Patient,* but this is a New Orleans favorite despite many historical inaccuracies.

Percy, Walker. *Lancelot.* New York: Farrar, Straus and Giroux, 1977.
    The Last Gentleman. New York: Farrar, Straus and Giroux, 1966.
    Love in the Ruins. New York: Farrar, Straus and Giroux, 1971.
    The Message in the Bottle. Farrar, Straus & Giroux, 1975 paperback.
    The Moviegoer. New York: Alfred A. Knopf, 1961.
    The Second Coming. New York: Farrar, Straus and Giroux, 1980.
    The Thanatos Syndrome. New York: Farrar, Straus and Giroux, 1987.

Percy's novels, complex and philosophical, were explorations of the ongoing struggle between faith and doubt, as well as landmarks of the sensibility of the New South. His struggle against despair and illness and toward an authentic Catholic faith struck a responsive chord with many readers. *The Moviegoer* is one of the novels most strongly associated with New Orleans, and Percy tapped into an entire generation's angst when he articulated Binx Bolling's devotion to "the search." In his later years, in such works as *The Message in the Bottle* and *Lost in the Cosmos,* Percy began to articulate a philosophy of language as well, asserting that language is at the very heart of our humanity.

Piazza, Tom. *Blues and Trouble.* New York: St. Martin's, 1996.
    An impressive debut collection of short stories from the well-known music critic.

Porter, Katherine Anne. *Collected Stories.* New York: Harcourt Brace, 1979.
    Letters of Katherine Anne Porter. New York: Grove-Atlantic, 1981.
    Porter is primarily regarded as a Texas writer, but her time in

New Orleans was obviously important to her, and her letters from the city are lovely and evocative.

Porter, William Sydney. *See* Henry, O.

Rechy, John. *City of Night.* Grove-Atlantic, 1988 paperback.
A novel about a homosexual hustler, part of which is set in New Orleans during Mardi Gras.

Redmann, Jean. *Death by the Riverside.* New Victoria Publications, paperback.
Deaths of Jocasta. New Victoria Publications, 1992 paperback.
Intersection of Law and Desire. Avon, 1997 paperback.
Lost Daughters. New York: W. W. Norton, 1999.
Redmann's mystery series centers on the lesbian detective Micky Knight.

Rhodes, Jewell Parker. *Voodoo Dreams: A Novel of Marie Laveau.* New York: St. Martin's, 1995 paperback.
A historical novel by a new African American writer.

Rice, Anne.
Cry to Heaven. New York: Knopf, 1982. Available in many editions.
The Feast of All Saints. New York: Simon & Schuster, 1979.
Interview with the Vampire. New York: Knopf, 1976.
Lasher. New York: Knopf, 1993.
Memnoch the Devil. New York: Knopf, 1995.
The Mummy, or Ramses the Damned. New York: Ballantine, 1989.
The Queen of the Damned. New York: Knopf, 1988.
Servant of the Bones. New York: Knopf, 1996.
The Tale of the Body Thief. New York: Knopf, 1992.
Taltos. New York: Knopf, 1994.
The Vampire Armand. New York: Knopf, 1998.
The Vampire Lestat. New York: Knopf, 1985.
Violin. New York: Knopf, 1997.

The Witching Hour. New York: Knopf, 1990.
(As Anne Rampling)
    Belinda. New York: Arbor House, 1986.
    Exit to Eden. New York: Arbor House, 1985.
(As A. N. Roquelaure)
    Beauty's Punishment. New York: Dutton, 1984.
    Beauty's Release. New York: Dutton, 1985.
    The Claiming of Sleeping Beauty. New York: Dutton, 1983.

Rice's long and successful writing career began with the publication of *Interview with the Vampire* in 1976. Her vampires, seductive, otherworldly talkative types, endlessly struggling with questions of morality and immortality, hit home with everyone who has ever felt like an outsider. Later, Rice began a series of books about a New Orleans family of witches called the Mayfairs, which has continued for several volumes. She has said that she wrote the A. N. Roquelaure books when she couldn't find the kind of pornography that she wanted to read, but most readers will find them fairly conventional. The Anne Rampling books are mainstream contemporary novels, written in what Rice calls her "American voice"; *Belinda* is a particularly revealing book about what it means to an artist to tell the truth about his work. Rice has also periodically turned to historical fiction: *The Feast of All Saints* is a novel about the free people of color in New Orleans and *Cry to Heaven* is a story of the Italian castrati. *Violin,* set in New Orleans, is a highly autobiographical novel about human grief and suffering after the death of loved ones.

Robbins, Tom. *Jitterbug Perfume.* New York: Bantam, 1984.
    You can visit Hove Parfumeur on Bourbon Street for a whiff of the inspiration Robbins found for his novel in New Orleans.

Sallis, James.
    Black Hornet. New York: Carroll & Graf, 1994.
    Bluebottle. New York, Walker, 1999.
    The Eye of the Cricket. New York: Walker, 1997.
    The Long-Legged Fly. New York: Carroll & Graf, 1992.
    Moth. New York: Carroll & Graf, 1993.

These are all in Sallis's detective series featuring Lew Griffin, an African American who is a literature professor at Tulane University.

Sancton, Thomas. *By Starlight*. Garden City, N.Y.: Doubleday, 1960.

Count Roller Skates. Garden City, N.Y.: Doubleday, 1956.

These two novels by a New Orleans native and a reporter for the New Orleans *Item* capture the underworld of the 1930s and 1940s. In a copy of *Count Roller Skates,* inscribed in May 1971, Sancton wrote, "I look back on those blocks of Canal Street, from 'Carl'ton to the Cemeteries,' in the 1920s and 1930s, as a wondrous imperishable village which had all the elements of the Great Globe itself, and all the human types by which I judged all others through life."

Shaik, Fatima. *The Mayor of New Orleans: Just Talking Jazz*. Berkeley: Creative Arts Books, 1989.

Three novellas by a native New Orleanian and former writer for the *Times- Picayune.*

Skinner, Robert. *Cat-Eyed Trouble*. New York: Kensington, 1997.

Skin Deep and Blood Red. New York: Kensington, 1996.

Skinner sets his series featuring African American detective Wesley Farrell in the New Orleans of the 1930s.

Smith, Julie. *The Axeman's Jazz*. New York: St. Martin's, 1991.

Crescent City Kill. New York: Fawcett, 1997.

82 Desire. New York: Fawcett Columbine, 1998.

House of Blues. New York: Ballantine, 1995.

Jazz Funeral. New York: Fawcett, 1993.

The Kindness of Strangers. New York: Ballantine, 1996.

New Orleans Beat. New York: Ballantine, 1994.

New Orleans Mourning. New York: St. Martin's, 1990.

Julie Smith's series featuring New Orleans policewoman Skip Langdon has taken on such topics as murder at Mardi Gras, murder in 12-step programs, and murder on the Internet.

Spencer, Elizabeth. *The Snare.* Louisiana State University Press Voices of the South series, 1994.

A remarkable New Orleans novel by one of the South's leading writers.

Stone, Robert. *Hall of Mirrors.* Viking Penguin, 1987 paperback.

This novel about a down-on-his-luck disk jockey named Rheinhardt in the New Orleans of the 1960s was nominated for a PEN/Faulkner Award and was later made into the movie *WUSA*.

Toole, John Kennedy. *Confederacy of Dunces.* Baton Rouge: Louisiana State University Press, 1980.

This New Orleans classic, winner of the Pulitzer Prize for fiction in 1981, hilariously captures the sounds and tastes and smells of real Crescent City life.

Twain, Mark. *Life on the Mississippi.* Boston: J. R. Osgood, 1883.

The classic of river life.

Wells, Rebecca. *Divine Secrets of the Ya-Ya Sisterhood.* New York: HarperCollins, 1996.

Little Altars Everywhere. Seattle: Broken Moon Press, 1992.

Wells, from Alexandria, Louisiana, writes about strong southern women and their struggles with work and love. She received the Western States Book Award for *Little Altars Everywhere. Divine Secrets of the Ya-Ya Sisterhood,* a best-selling novel about lifelong female friends who call themselves the Ya-Yas, inspired Ya-Ya sisterhood groups around the country.

Wilcox, James. *Guest of a Sinner.* New York: HarperCollins, 1993.

Miss Undine's Living Room. New York: Harper & Row, 1987.

Modern Baptists. New York: Dial Press, 1983.

North Gladiola. New York: Harper & Row, 1985.

Plain and Normal. New York: Little, Brown, 1998.

Polite Sex. New York: HarperCollins, 1991.

Sort of Rich. New York: Harper & Row, 1989.

Wilcox's stories of the denizens of Tula Springs, Louisiana, are witty, underappreciated wonders. He recently received a considerable amount of unwanted attention when a *New Yorker* profile cited him as a dramatic case of a talented American writer who was unable to make a decent living from his work. Wilcox, a Louisiana native, now lives in New York, where much of his most recent work is set. His later comedies of domestic manners often describe Louisianians adrift in Manhattan.

Williams, Tennessee. *The Collected Stories.* New York: New Directions, 1985.
A Streetcar Named Desire. New York: New Directions, 1947.
Suddenly Last Summer. New York: New Directions, 1958.
Vieux Carre. New York: New Directions, 1979.
Tennessee Williams is synonymous with New Orleans even though he was born in Mississippi and used the city primarily as a refuge. His heartbroken, tormented southerners are among the most memorable characters associated with the city.

Wiltz, Christine. *A Diamond before You Die.* New York: Warner Books, 1988.
The Emerald Lizard. New York: Dutton, 1991.
Glass House. Baton Rouge: Louisiana State University Press, 1994.
The Killing Circle. New York: Macmillan, 1981.
Wiltz is the creator of the Neal Rafferty detective series, one of the grittiest, most realistic ever set in the city. In 1994, she turned her attention to the pressing problems of race relations in *Glass House,* a tough-minded, realistic novel based on a real incident of police brutality.

Woodward, Margaret. *No Place to Call Home.* New York: Fawcett, 1997 paperback original.
Still Waters. New York: G. P. Putnam's Sons, 1994 (published in a 1996 paperback reprint by Ballantine as *The Indictment*).
Woodward, a New Orleans attorney, began her writing career with *Still Waters,* a courtroom drama set in a Mobile that very much resembles New Orleans. *No Place to Call Home* is a novel

about a young boy who finds himself in foster care and the adults who become involved in his life.

BELLES LETTRES, HISTORY, MEMOIRS, BIOGRAPHIES

Ball, Edward. *Slaves in the Family.* New York: Farrar, Straus & Giroux, 1998.

In this remarkable book, Ball, whose family has deep roots in Louisiana, traces the lives of his slave-owning ancestors, their slaves, and the occasionally racially mixed descendants of his family, the Balls of South Carolina.

Barry, John. *Rising Tide: The Great Mississippi Flood of 1927 and How It Changed America.* New York: Simon & Schuster, 1997.

Journalist/historian Barry has written a page-turner of a history book that illuminates a compelling chapter in the New Orleans's past, when city fathers chose to dynamite the downstream levees and flood the land of poorer Louisianians in order to save themselves, an act that was eventually found to be unnecessary. Barry's look at New Orleans society of the late 1920s is fascinating, as is his view of the prominent Percy family and its role in this particular crisis and in southern history in general.

Basso, Etolia S. *The World from Jackson Square.* New York: Farrar Straus, 1948.

This lovely collection by a New Orleans native, with an introduction by her husband, the writer Hamilton Basso, is a wonderful anthology of impressions of New Orleans, part of the City and Country Reader series published by Farrar, Straus. It includes works by Charles Gayarré, Lyle Saxon, George Washington Cable, Walt Whitman, Mark Twain, William Faulkner, Lafcadio Hearn, John Galsworthy, and John Dos Passos. Search out an original in one of the city's used bookstores; it's a treasure.

Bates, Randolph. *Rings: On the Life and Family of a Southern Fighter.* New York: Farrar, Straus & Giroux, 1992.

Bates, who is white, found himself in many unexpected places as a result of following the career of Collis Phillips, a black man who struggled to support his family through boxing. A searching meditation on class and race by a wonderful writer.

Bisland, Elizabeth. *The Life and Letters of Lafcadio Hearn*. Boston: Houghton, Mifflin, 1906.
   The first full-length study of Hearn.

Boggs, Lindy. *Washington through a Purple Veil: Memoirs of a Southern Woman*. New York: Harcourt Brace, 1994.
   The former congresswoman recounts her remarkable life in this autobiography, which touches on many of the important moments not only in Louisiana history, but in our nation's modern history as well.

Brown, Dorothy H., and Barbara C. Ewell, eds. *Louisiana Women Writers: New Essays and a Comprehensive Bibliography*. Baton Rouge: Louisiana State University Press, 1992.
   Though now somewhat outdated, this is a landmark volume, with twelve critical essays.

Bryan, Violet Harrington. *The Myth of New Orleans in Literature: Dialogues of Race and Gender*. Knoxville: University of Tennessee Press, 1993.
   A groundbreaking study by one of the city's leading African American scholars of the work of George Washington Cable, Grace King, Alice Dunbar-Nelson, Marcus Christian, Tom Dent, Brenda Marie Osbey, and Tennessee Williams.

Codrescu, Andrei. *The Dog with the Chip in His Neck: Essays from NPR and Elsewhere*. New York: St. Martin's, 1996.
   Hail Babylon! In Search of the American City at the End of the Millennium. New York: St. Martin's, 1998.
   The Muse Is Always Half-Dressed in New Orleans and Other Essays. New York: St. Martin's, 1993.
   Road Scholar: Coast to Coast Late in the Century. New York: Hyperion, 1993.
   Zombification: Stories from NPR. New York: St. Martin's, 1994.

Codrescu's commentary for National Public Radio is idiosyncratic and amusing, often with a twist of insight that could only come from his unique perspective as an outsider with a poet's sensibility. His writing about New Orleans is always on target and affectionate. *Road Scholar* is his account of the coast-to-coast road trip chronicled in the award-winning film of the same name. *Hail Babylon!* is a collection of his travel writing and includes a memorable piece about New Orleans.

Cott, Jonathan. *Wandering Ghost: The Odyssey of Lafcadio Hearn.* New York: Alfred A. Knopf, 1990.
    This is my favorite Hearn biography, beautifully written, with substantial quotations from his work.

Cowan, Walter, John Wilds, and Charles L. Dufour. *Louisiana, Yesterday and Today.* Baton Rouge: Louisiana State University Press, 1996.
Cowan, Walter, O. K. LeBlanc, John C. Chase, John Wilds, and Charles L. Dufour. *New Orleans Yesterday and Today.* Baton Rouge: Louisiana State University Press, 1983, rev. ed. 1988.
    Two excellent introductions to city and state history by veteran newspapermen.

De Caro, Frank, ed., and Rosan Augusta Jordan, assoc. ed. *Louisiana Sojourns: Travelers' Tales and Literary Journeys.* Baton Rouge: Louisiana State University Press, 1998.
    This is the perfect book to read in preparation for a trip to Louisiana or to browse through while you're here. Readers have the sweet sensation of traveling through time, as well as in the footsteps of seventy-six remarkable traveler writers, from Spanish explorers to contemporary writers such as Calvin Trillin. There are sections devoted to the Mississippi River, New Orleans, plantations, festivals, the African American presence, the Civil War, Cajun country, central and north Louisiana, the bayous, marshes, and coast, wildlife and the natural environment, and the world of the spirits. "Travel Updates" appear at the end of every chapter with useful information for contemporary visitors. De Caro is a professor at LSU.

Dent, Thomas. *Southern Journey: A Return to the Civil Rights Movement.* New York: William Morrow, 1997.

Dent, a poet and founder of the Free Southern Theater and a former aide to UN ambassador Andrew Young, here chronicles his return to many of the sites throughout the South that were crucial in the civil rights movement, describing what has changed and what has remained the same.

Desdunes, Rodolphe Lucien. *Our People and Our History: A Tribute to the Creole People of Color.* Ed. Sister Dorothea Olga Mc-Cants. Baton Rouge, Louisiana State University Press, 1973.

First published in French in 1911, this book was written by a Creole of color and includes extensive political, cultural, and social information.

Dubus, Andre. *Meditations from a Movable Chair.* New York: Alfred A. Knopf, 1998.

This collection of essays touches a bit on Dubus's experiences in his native Louisiana. A particularly powerful reflection, "Digging," describes the summer he was sixteen, working on a construction crew in Lafayette, struggling to become a man. He lived most of his adult life in Massachusetts. These twelve essays also describe his life after he was crippled by a hit-and-run driver while helping stranded motorists in 1986, also the subject of his 1990 essay collection *Broken Vessels.*

Evans, Oliver. *New Orleans.* New York: Macmillan, 1959.
A delightful history of the city by a friend of Tennessee Williams.

Ewell, Barbara. *Kate Chopin.* New York: Ungar, 1986.
A critical work by a Loyola University professor of English.

Feibleman, Peter. *Lilly: Reminiscences of Lillian Hellman.* New York: William Morrow, 1988.
Feibleman discusses his years with Hellman, late in her life.

Gayarré, Charles. *History of Louisiana.* Gretna, La.: Pelican, 1974.

A reprint of the classic four-volume history, originally published in the mid-1800s.

Griffin, John Howard. *Black Like Me*. Boston: Houghton Mifflin, 1961.

When Griffin, a white writer, set out to transform himself into a black man and experience black life in America, he began his journey in New Orleans.

Hearn, Lafcadio. *Chita: A Memory of Last Island*. New York: Harper Brothers, 1889.

"Gombo Zhebes": A Little Dictionary of Creole Proverbs. New York: Will H. Coleman, 1885.

Sketch Book Guide to New Orleans and Environs. New York: Will H. Coleman, 1885.

Hearn is one of the most interesting characters in all New Orleans literature, but little of his work is currently in print.

Hellman, Lillian. *Six Plays by Lillian Hellman: The Children's Hour, Days to Come, The Little Foxes, Watch on the Rhine, Another Part of the Forest, The Autumn Garden*. New York: Modern Library, 1960.

Three: An Unfinished Woman, Pentimento, Scoundrel Time. Boston: Little, Brown, 1979.

These collected works give a sense of the range of Hellman's work; look for New Orleans settings in *The Children's Hour* and *An Unfinished Woman*.

Hirsch, Arnold R., and Joseph Logsdon, eds. *Creole New Orleans: Race and Americanization*. Baton Rouge: Louisiana State University Press, 1992.

An invaluable collection of essays that explore the complex ethnic makeup of the city.

Holl, Shelley N. C. *Louisiana Dayride: 52 Short Trips from New Orleans*. Jackson: University Press of Mississippi, 1995.

Holl, who has written for the Lagniappe entertainment section of the *Times-Picayune,* here collects the best short day trips from the city.

Jumonville, Florence. *Bibliography of New Orleans Imprints, 1764–1864.* New Orleans: Historic New Orleans Collection, 1989.
   The ultimate guide to printing and publishing in this city through the Civil War.

Kemp, John R. *New Orleans: An Illustrated History.* Sun Valley, Calif.: American Historical Press, 1997.
   This is an updated version of an earlier volume, a good basic history with well-chosen vintage illustrations.

Kennedy, Richard S., ed. *Literary New Orleans: Essays and Meditations.* Baton Rouge: Louisiana State University Press, 1992.
   Literary New Orleans in the Modern World. Baton Rouge: Louisiana State University Press, 1998.
   Two essential and accessible collections of critical essays by noted scholars.

King, Grace. *Creole Families of New Orleans.* New York: Macmillan, 1921 (reprint Baton Rouge: Claitor's, 1971).
   Memories of a Southern Woman of Letters. New York: Macmillan, 1932 (reprint, New York: Ayer, 1977).
   New Orleans: The Place and the People. New York: Macmillan, 1895.
   Nonfiction by one of New Orleans's leading women writers.

Kirkwood, James. *American Grotesque.* New York: Simon & Schuster, 1970.
   Kirkwood's account of the prosecution of Clay Shaw for his alleged part in the assassination of John F. Kennedy, largely found to be a witch hunt by District Attorney Jim Garrison.

Laborde, Errol. *The Buzzard Wore a Tutu: Chronicles of Life and Adventures in New Orleans.* New Orleans: Urban Press, 1994.
   I Never Danced with an Eggplant on a Streetcar Before. New Orleans: Urban Press, 1988.

Laborde, editor of *New Orleans Magazine,* is a veteran journalist and native New Orleanian. These two volumes collect his columns and essays, lovely little slices of New Orleans life.

Leverich, Lyle. *Tom: The Unknown Tennessee Williams.* New York: Crown, 1995.
Leverich, who gained access to previously unavailable material, is at work on the second volume of this authorized biography, which will probably stand as the definitive critical life of the playwright.

Macdonald, Robert R., John R. Kemp, and Edward F. Haas, eds. *Louisiana's Black Heritage.* New Orleans: Louisiana State Museum, 1979.
Excellent essays.

Marcus, Jana. *In the Shadow of the Vampire: Reflections on the World of Anne Rice.* New York: Thunder's Mouth Press, 1997.
Marcus, a freelance photographer and documentary filmmaker, came to New Orleans for the Coven Ball at Halloween and found herself fascinated by the fans of Rice's work. This book tells their stories.

Mardis, James. *Kente Cloth: Southwest Voices of the African Diaspora.* Denton, Texas: University of North Texas Press, 1998.
This anthology includes pieces by forty-five writers, mostly from Louisiana and Texas, including many New Orleans writers.

Marks, Leta Weiss. *Time's Tapestry: Four Generations of a New Orleans Family.* Baton Rouge: Louisiana State University Press, 1997.
Marks describes what it was like growing up Jewish in New Orleans in the 1940s, in a book flavored with an insider's view of the politics of the period. Her father was Huey Long's chosen architect and created many of the state's most important landmarks, including the New State Capitol and Charity Hospital. He was indicted and served jail time during the "Louisiana Hayride" scandals.

Martinez, Elsie, and Margaret LeCorgne. *Uptown/Downtown: Growing Up in New Orleans.* Lafayette: University of Southwestern Louisiana Center for Louisiana Studies, 1986.

A lovely little memoir of growing up in New Orleans in the 1930s.

McCaffety, Kerri. *Obituary Cocktail: The Great Saloons of New Orleans.* New Orleans: Pontalba Press, 1998.

Photographer and trained anthropologist Kerri McCaffety examines the drinking culture of New Orleans in one of the best books about the city. She explores nearly fifty bars and saloons in approximately two hundred color photographs. Whether you're drawn to the history of the Napoleon House, the poetic ambiance of the Maple Leaf Bar, or the elegance of the Sazerac Bar at the Fairmont, you'll find something here to raise your spirits. As a bonus, there's a drink recipe from each establishment. Voted Book of the Year for 1998 by the New Orleans Gulf South Booksellers Association.

Pinckley, Diana, with corporate profiles by Garry Boulard and Elizabeth Donze and photographs by Jackson Hill/Southern Lights studio. *New Orleans: River Region Renaissance.* Montgomery, Ala.: Community Communications, 1996.

Commissioned by the Chamber of Commerce, this is a great look at contemporary New Orleans, from its business climate to its artistic life. Longtime Orleanian Pinckley's fast-paced prose makes for easy, informative reading and Hill's photography is wonderful. (Disregard the advertorials at the back.)

Plimpton, George, ed. *Truman Capote: In Which Various Friends, Enemies, Acquaintances, and Detractors Recall His Turbulent Career.* New York: Doubleday, 1997.

This fascinating oral biography gives new insight into Capote's life and troubled genius, but not much about New Orleans.

Prejean, Helen. *Dead Man Walking: An Eyewitness Account of the Death Penalty in the United States.* New York: Random House, 1993.

This is Prejean's best-selling account of her vigils with convicts on Angola's death row.

Ramsland, Katherine. *Prism of the Night: A Biography of Anne Rice.* New York: Dutton, 1991.
Rutgers University professor Ramsland, long an Anne Rice fan, here has produced the first real biography of Rice, with the author's cooperation. Illuminating, but somewhat adoring in tone.

Roberts, Cokie. *We Are Our Mothers' Daughters.* New York: William Morrow, 1998.
This best-selling memoir by the journalist and daughter of Lindy Boggs, former congresswoman and now ambassador to the Vatican, is a meditation on women's roles, as well as a lovely memoir of growing up in a family of strong Louisiana women.

Rogers, Kim Lacy. *Righteous Lives: Narratives of the New Orleans Civil Rights Movement.* New York: New York University Press, 1993.
A revealing look at the lives of leading New Orleans civil rights activists.

ya Salaam, Kalamu. *What Is Life? Reclaiming the Black Blues Self.* Chicago: Third World, 1994 paperback original.
This is a collection of essays on race and identity by one of New Orleans's leading writers.

Samway, Patrick. *Walker Percy: A Life.* New York: Farrar, Straus & Giroux, 1997.
This biography is by a Percy scholar who is also a Jesuit priest and editor of *America* magazine.

Sayer, Mandy. *Dreamtime Alice: A Memoir.* New York: Ballantine Books, 1998.
This memoir is by an Australian Alice-in-Wonderland who followed her father to the world of street performing in New York

and New Orleans. Ever wonder what the lives of those street musicians you see in the French Quarter are really like? Sayer's book describes how tough and sordid, yet how seductive, it can be. (Sayer is married to Pulitzer Prize–winning poet Yusef Komunyakaa.)

Spencer, Elizabeth. *Landscapes of the Heart: A Memoir.* New York: Random House, 1998.
  The distinguished southern novelist here recalls a now-vanished South, with a brief account of her time in New Orleans working on her novel *The Snare.*

Spoto, Donald. *The Kindness of Strangers: The Life of Tennessee Williams.* Boston: Little, Brown, 1985.
  One of the early biographies of Williams, by a celebrity journalist.

Strahan, Jerry E. *Managing Ignatius: The Lunacy of Lucky Dogs and Life in the Quarter.* Baton Rouge: Louisiana State University Press, 1998.
  This hilarious memoir is a must for anyone who's curious about French Quarter culture, as well as for any fan of *A Confederacy of Dunces.* Strahan, longtime manager of Lucky Dogs, Inc., is also a scholar and the author of *Andrew Jackson Higgins and the Boats That Won World War II,* about the New Orleans–based creator of the craft that made possible the D-Day landing on the beaches at Normandy in 1944.

Tolson, Jay. *Pilgrim in the Ruins: A Life of Walker Percy.* New York: Simon & Schuster, 1992.
  Tolson is the editor of the *Wilson Quarterly,* and this, one of the first biographies of Percy, is a model of restraint and intelligence.

Toth, Emily. *Kate Chopin: A Life.* New York: William Morrow, 1990. (University of Texas Press, 1995 paperback.)
  Unveiling Kate Chopin. Jackson: University Press of Mississippi, 1999.

Toth, a professor of English at LSU, is a longtime Chopin scholar; these readable books reflect her expertise as well as her ability to capture the reader's attention.

Upton, Dell, ed. *Madaline: Love and Survival in Antebellum New Orleans*. Athens: University of Georgia Press, 1996.
The memoirs, newly rediscovered and edited, of a kept woman, Madaline Selima Edwards.

Virgets, Ronnie. *Say, Cap! The New Orleans Views of Ronnie Virgets*. New Orleans: Arthur Hardy Enterprises, 1997.
Virgets, a native and a journalist, collects his humorous anecdotes for the *Times-Picayune* and for *Gambit* in this volume.

Williams, Tennessee. *Memoirs*. Garden City, N.Y.: Doubleday, 1975.
Generally acknowledged not to be Williams's best work (he wrote it for some quick cash), this is nevertheless an interesting, if sketchy, look at his experiences in New Orleans.

Wiltz, Christine. *The Last Madam: A Life in the New Orleans Underworld*. New York; Faber and Faber/Farrar, Straus & Giroux, 1999.
This is a fascinating look at the life and times of Norma Wallace, who ran the last of the legendary houses of prostitution in the French Quarter, post-Storyville.

Winik, Marion. *First Comes Love*. New York: Pantheon, 1996.
Winik, a commentator for National Public Radio, describes her marriage to a gay man and his death from AIDS in this tough and affecting memoir, partly set in New Orleans, where they met.

Wonk, Dalt. *French Quarter Fables*. New Orleans: Temperance Hall, 1993.
Riddles of Existence. New Orleans: Temperance Hall, 1996.
New Fables. New Orleans: self-published, 1997.
Wonk writes and illustrates his fables and riddles for grown-ups, all with a distinctive New Orleans flavor.

Wyatt-Brown, Bertram. *The House of Percy: Honor, Melancholy, and Imagination in a Southern Family.* New York: Oxford University Press, 1994.

This scholarly biography describes the life and times of one of the most prominent of southern families, dogged by a sense of duty and haunted by family tragedy.

ART AND ARCHITECTURE

Arrigo, Joseph. *Louisiana's Plantation Homes: The Grace and Grandeur.* Stillwater, Minn.: Voyageur Press, 1991.

A lovely tour of the River Road in pen-and-ink sketches and photographs.

Benfey, Christopher. *Degas in New Orleans: Encounters in the Creole World of Kate Chopin and George Washington Cable.* New York: Alfred A. Knopf, 1997.

Despite many factual errors, this is an interesting look at New Orleans society in 1872, when Edgar Degas came to New Orleans for a visit between All Saints Day and Mardi Gras.

Bookhardt, D. Eric, and Jon Newlin. *Geopsychic Wonders of New Orleans.* New Orleans: Temperance Hall, 1992.

This is an idiosyncratic and amazing view of New Orleans landmarks that are all too often overlooked. Bookhardt is the art critic for *Gambit,* and Newlin is a native New Orleanian, bookseller, and writer.

Brady, Patricia, Louise C. Hoffman, and Lynn D. Adams, eds. *Complementary Visions of Louisiana Art: The Laura Simon Nelson Collection at the Historic New Orleans Collection.* New Orleans: Historic New Orleans Collection, 1996.

Comprehensive look at Louisiana art and its place in American art history by critics and historians, with beautiful reproductions.

Cable, Mary. *Lost New Orleans.* Foreword by Samuel Wilson. Boston: Houghton Mifflin, 1980.

A look at the city's architectural past.

Chase, John. *Frenchmen, Desire, Good Children, and Other Streets of New Orleans.* New Orleans: Robert L. Crager, 1949.

This is a must for any New Orleans reading list, the definitive history of New Orleans street names by the late editorial cartoonist for the *Times-Picayune*.

Christian, Marcus. *Negro Ironworkers in Louisiana, 1718–1900.* Gretna, La.: Pelican, 1972.

Marcus Christian directed the Negro Unit of the Federal Writers Project at Dillard University.

Clark, Sandra Russell. *Elysium—A Gathering of Souls: New Orleans Cemeteries.* Foreword by Andrei Codrescu. Introduction by Patricia Brady. Baton Rouge: Louisiana State University Press, 1997.

This is a collection of gorgeous photographs of cemeteries, along with carefully selected literary quotations. Patricia Brady contributes an enlightening introduction describing New Orleans burial customs, while Codrescu entertains with his thoughts on cemeteries—as coffeehouses or as places to lose one's virginity.

Delehanty, Randolph. *Art of the American South: Works from the Ogden Collection.* Baton Rouge: Louisiana State University Press, 1996.

Art historian Delehanty here provides a glimpse into the works of the Roger Ogden collection, along with a fascinating introduction about the history of southern art in general and New Orleans art in particular.

Feigenbaum, Gail, and Jean Sutherland Boggs. *Degas and New Orleans: A French Impressionist in America.* New York, Rizzoli, 1999.

Written to accompany the 1999 "Degas in New Orleans" exhibit at the New Orleans Museum of Art, this book includes essays and sixty full-color and eighty black-and-white illustrations.

Florence, Robert, text; Mason Florence, photographs. *New Orleans*

On the other side of Rampart, my mother smiles nervously as we pass beneath the rusted wrought-iron gates to the cemetery.

"All hope abandon," Cora says. . . .

"We're just asking for it," my sister says. "And we've got the perfect guide."

Bobbie stops to unfold her directions on one of the shattered marbles. She examines the waiter's drawing then points in the general direction of the housing project.

"It says that way."

The bleached crypts reflect the sun like sheets on a clothesline. Everything's broken: the slanted crosses, the stone slabs, the endless stacked vaults. It's a small city of crumbling stucco and brick.

Bobbie glances at her map every few feet and leads my mother down another row of tombs. Many of the larger crypts contain several generations that go back hundreds of years.

"The one place I can see a family staying together," Cora says.

—James Gordon Bennett, *The Moon Stops Here*

Cemeteries: Life in the Cities of the Dead. New Orleans: Batture Press, 1997.

Robert Florence's substantial text about the history and the life surrounding New Orleans cemeteries is complemented by the color photographs of his brother, Mason Florence.

Friedlander, Lee. *E. J. Bellocq.* New York: Random House, 1996.

A collection of the photographs of E. J. Bellocq, this is a fascinating blend of the sacred and the profane, from communion pictures to the well-known portraits of the women of Storyville.

Friends of the Cabildo. *New Orleans Architecture.* Gretna, La.: Pelican, various dates.

This landmark eight-volume series includes *The Lower Garden District,* Vol. I; *The American Sector,* Volume II; *The Cemeteries,* Vol. III; *The Creole Faubourgs,* Vol. IV; *The Esplanade Ridge,* Vol. V; *Faubourg Tremé and the Bayou Road,* Vol. VI; *Jefferson City,* Vol. VII; and *The University Section,* Vol. VIII. This comprehensive inventory of New Orleans buildings was undertaken by the Friends of the Cabildo.

Genthe, Arnold. *Impressions of Old New Orleans.* Foreword by Grace King. New York: George H. Doran, 1926.

Gorgeous photographs of old New Orleans. Very expensive and hard to find now.

Gould, Philip, and Larry Powell. *Louisiana's Capitols: The Power and the Beauty.* Lafayette: Galerie Press, 1995.

There are two capitol buildings in Baton Rouge: the castlelike Old State Capitol beside the Mississippi River, and the skyscraper New State Capitol built under the proud eye of Huey P. Long. Gould's beautiful photographs and Powell's smart text illuminate the two buildings—and a lot about Louisiana politics as well.

Guste, Roy Jr. *Secret Gardens of the Vieux Carre.* Boston: Little, Brown, 1993.

Ever wonder what's behind all those doors and gates in the French Quarter, hidden from view? This gorgeous book, unfortunately now out of print, gives you a tantalizing glimpse.

Heard, Malcolm. *French Quarter Manual.* Jackson: University Press of Mississippi, 1997.

A must for anyone interested in New Orleans architecture. Heard, a professor of architecture at Tulane University, gives readers the tools to see the Quarter—illuminating essays about the types of buildings and building components, all illustrated with vintage photographs and complemented by quotations from other writers.

Lane, Mills. *Architecture of the Old South: Louisiana.* Photographs by Van Jones Martin. Savannah: Beehive Press, 1997.

This volume, part of a ten-book series, is a reissue of an earlier work (published by Abbeville Press in 1990), and includes old photographs and drawings, as well as contemporary photographs.

Laughlin, Clarence John. *Ghosts along the Mississippi.* New York: Scribner's Sons, 1948.

This is Laughlin's most famous work, in which he set out to document a vanishing way of life. His surreal photographs of decaying mansions do seem haunted, sad, and lovely.

Lawrence, John H., and Brady, Patricia. *Haunter of Ruins: The Photography of Clarence John Laughlin.* New York: Bulfinch, 1997.

This book draws on the Historic New Orleans Collection's archive of Laughlin's work, along with essays by such writers as Ellen Gilchrist, Andrei Codrescu, Shirley Ann Grau, and Jonathan Williams.

Lockwood, C. C. *Atchafalaya.* Baton Rouge: Louisiana State University Press, 1984.

Lockwood, one of Louisiana's outstanding nature photographers, here documents the great swampland of the Atchafalaya Basin.

Mahe, John, Rosanne McCaffrey, and Patricia Brady. *Encyclopedia of New Orleans Artists, 1718–1918*. New Orleans: Historic New Orleans Collection, 1987.

Information on more than 2,200 artists and art organizations active in the city.

Mitchell, William Jr., with photographs by James A. Lockhart. *Classic New Orleans*. Savannah: Golden Coast, 1993.

A rather staid look at the great houses of New Orleans.

Poesch, Jessie, and Barbara SoRelle Bacot, eds. *Louisiana Buildings, 1720–1940: The Historic American Buildings Survey*. Baton Rouge: Louisiana State University Press, 1997.

This fascinating volume is the product of a federal program that began during the Great Depression. It identifies and documents hundreds of buildings of different types, and there are scholarly essays on a number of topics by preservationists, architectural historians, and art historians.

Seidenberg, Charlotte. *The New Orleans Garden*. Jackson: University Press of Mississippi, 1993.

One of the few books devoted exclusively to New Orleans gardens, Seidenberg's is a handy how-to book that is filled with great garden stories as well.

Sexton, Richard, and Randolph Delehanty. *New Orleans: Elegance and Decadence*. San Francisco: Chronicle Books, 1993.

One of the best books ever done on the city, this is a gorgeous look at the defining twin themes of elegance and decadence, with glorious photographs by Sexton and a well-written text by Delehanty. The perfect souvenir, it belongs on every New Orleans bookshelf.

Sims, Julia. *Manchac Swamp: Louisiana's Undiscovered Wilderness*. Introduction by John Kemp. Baton Rouge: Louisiana State University Press, 1996.

Sims, who found solace in the swamp after the deaths of her father and brother, here collects her beautiful photographs of this mysterious landscape, so close to New Orleans, yet so hard to get to. Kemp's introduction gives us a history of the area as well as a look at the way people live in the swamp today. This is an affecting portrait of a vanishing landscape and way of life.

Spielman, David, photographs, and William Starr, text. *Southern Writers*. Columbia, S.C.: University of South Carolina Press, 1997.

Spielman, a Mandeville photographer, captures a gallery of southern writers in this collection, including many from Louisiana—Anne Rice, Ernest Gaines, Shirley Ann Grau, and Christine Wiltz, to name a few.

Starr, S. Frederick. *Southern Comfort: The Garden District of New Orleans, 1800–1900*. Cambridge, Mass.: MIT Press, 1989 (reprinted by Chronicle Books, 1998.)

Starr, formerly a professor at Tulane University, is a great lover of New Orleans architecture and music. This is a grand tour of the Garden District, but beware, there are some mistakes in the information presented. The Chronicle Books reprint has gorgeous color photographs.

Sternberg, Mary Ann. *Along the River Road: Past and Present on Louisiana's Historic Byway*. Baton Rouge: Louisiana State University Press, 1996.

A wonderful guide to the state's best-known thoroughfare, with lots of historical information as well as illustrations.

Toledano, Roulhac. *The National Trust Guide to New Orleans*. New York: Wiley, 1996.

One of the most interesting and useful guides to city buildings, written by one of the editors of the New Orleans Architecture series.

Turner, Suzanne, text, and A. J. Meek, photographs. *Louisiana Gardens: Places of Work and Wonder*. Baton Rouge: Louisiana State University Press, 1997.

Turner, a professor of landscape architecture at Louisiana State University, and Meek, a photographer who also created the work

Red Pepper Paradise, about Avery Island, here show the range of Louisiana's public and private gardens. There are gorgeous full-color photographs and a text that describes each garden, as well as a fascinating overview of the state's horticultural history.

Vella, Christina. *Intimate Enemies: The Two Worlds of the Baroness de Pontalba.* Baton Rouge: Louisiana State University Press, 1997.

Vella, a Tulane professor of history, describes the fascinating life of the Baroness Micaela de Pontalba, who built New Orleans's famous Pontalba Buildings—an amazing woman who survived a murder attempt by her father-in-law and a disastrous marriage to pursue a career and a life played out on the world stage.

Vetter, Cyril. *Fonville Winans' Louisiana: Politics, People, and Places.* Baton Rouge: Louisiana State University Press, 1995.

A collection of images by one of the state's most interesting and discerning photographers; author Vetter provides biographical information and anecdotes.

MUSIC

Ancelet, Barry Jean. *Cajun Music: Its Origin and Development.* Lafayette: University of Southwest Louisiana Center for Louisiana Studies, 1989.

Ancelet is an authority on all things Cajun; this is an important work.

Ancelet, Barry Jean, and Elemore Morgan Jr. *The Makers of Cajun Music.* Austin: University of Texas Press, 1984.

An early study, now unfortunately out of print, worth seeking out.

Armstrong, Louis. *Satchmo: My Life in New Orleans.* New York: Prentice Hall, 1954 (paperback, New York: Da Capo, 1986).

This should be one of the classics of African American autobiography. Armstrong wrote all of his life, owned a typewriter, and signed his letters "Red beans and ricely yours."

Bechet, Sidney. *Treat It Gentle.* New York: Hill and Wang, 1960.
The autobiography of the great jazz clarinetist.

Bergreen, Laurence. *Louis Armstrong: An Extravagant Life.* New York: Riverhead, 1997.
This biographer had access to new archival material, and the work is fascinating reading, but there are so many factual errors, at least in the New Orleans sections, that it's unwise to rely on it as a sole source.

Bernard, Shane. *Swamp Pop: Cajun and Creole Rhythm and Blues.* Jackson: University Press of Mississippi, 1996.
Bernard's book is a useful history of one of Louisiana's major contributions to the roots of rock and roll.

Berrett, Joshua. *The Louis Armstrong Companion: Eight Decades of Commentary.* New York: Schirmer Books, 1999.
Collects eight decades of musical criticism of Armstrong's work and many of Armstrong's previously unpublished writings.

Berry, Jason, Jonathan Foose, and Tad Jones. *Up from the Cradle of Jazz: New Orleans Music since World War II.* Athens: University of Georgia Press, 1986.
One of the best books ever written on New Orleans music, tracing four decades of the art form and its leading figures, from Fats Domino to Professor Longhair, from the Neville Brothers to the Mardi Gras Indians.

Brady, Patricia, and Louise Hoffman, eds. *Jazz Scrapbook: Bill Russell and Some Highly Musical Friends.* New Orleans: Historic New Orleans Collection, 1998.
This collection of wonderful photographs and writings is from the Bill Russell Archive at the Historic New Orleans Collection. Russell, a jazz scholar who died in 1992, had a passion for the music and its performers. This informal scrapbook includes sections on Jelly Roll Morton, Bunk Johnson, Mahalia Jackson, drum-

mer Baby Dodds, trumpeter Natty Dominique, and piano man "Fess" Manetta. Russell wrote in 1951, "If a person really has the right kind of music in their mind, heart & body, they are likely to think and act right . . . be happy, love everyone and hate no one. . . . If all this sounds like a religion, I'm sorry, but until these ideas can be proven wrong, I'll go on believing." This is a fine tribute to a true New Orleans original.

Carter, William. *Preservation Hall: Music from the Heart*. New York: W. W. Norton, 1991.

Only in New Orleans could you get a full-length biography of a musical venue! Preservation Hall's history is an integral part of the city's musical and cultural heritage.

Friedlander, Lee. *The Jazz People of New Orleans*. New York: Pantheon Books, 1992.

Photographs of musicians.

Giddins, Gary. *Satchmo*. New York: Doubleday, 1988.

A biographical work, with lots of great photographs.

Goreau, Laurraine. *Just Mahalia, Baby: The Mahalia Jackson Story*. Waco: Word Books, 1975.

Biography of the great gospel singer, a New Orleans native who is also buried here.

Gould, Philip. *Cajun Music and Zydeco*. Baton Rouge: Louisiana State University Press, 1992.

Gould, one of Louisiana's premier photographers, here takes viewers on a musical journey through the sites of zydeco and Cajun music, with performers, dance halls and festivals galore. Barry Jean Ancelet's introduction provides a brief and useful history, and there is a CD with the same title.

Hannusch, Jeff. *I Hear You Knockin': The Sound of New Orleans Rhythm and Blues*. Ville Platte, La.: Swallow Publications, 1985.

One of the classic New Orleans music histories, which features profiles of more than thirty important figures.

John, Dr. (Mac Rebennack), with Jack Rummel. *Under a Hoodoo Moon: The Life of the Night Tripper.* New York: St. Martin's Press, 1994.
The autobiography of one of New Orleans's most famous musicians, this is particularly interesting for its chronicle of musical life in the city in the 1950s and 1960s.

Marquis, Don. *Finding Buddy Bolden: First Man of Jazz.* Louisiana State University Press, 1993 paperback.
In this reprint of a 1978 small press book, a jazz scholar discusses the elusive jazz trumpeter.

Marsalis, Wynton. *Marsalis on Music.* New York: W. W. Norton, 1995
Sweet Swing Blues on the Road. Photos by Frank Stewart. New York: W. W. Norton, 1994.
The Marsalis family is a mainstay of the New Orleans—and national—music scene. *Marsalis on Music* is a volume accompanying a series for public television introducing young people to music; *Sweet Swing Blues on the Road* is an evocative story of touring with a band.

Monceaux, Morgan. *Jazz: My Music My People.* New York: Alfred A. Knopf, 1994.
Originally published as a children's book, this volume is a treasure for all ages, with Monceaux's folk art portraits of jazz greats paired with fascinating, idiosyncratic biographical sketches.

Olivier, Rick, photographs, and Ben Sandmel, text. *Zydeco!* Jackson: University Press of Mississippi, 1999.
Eighty of Olivier's gorgeous black-and-white prints are accompanied by music writer Sandmel's text, a good introduction to zydeco music and culture.

Palmer, Robert. *Deep Blues*. New York: Viking Penguin, 1981.

Rock & Roll: An Unruly History. New York: Crown Publishing Group, 1995.

Palmer, one of the great music writers, lived in New Orleans off and on during the last years of his life. He died in 1997.

Piazza. Tom. *Blues Up and Down: Jazz in Our Time*. New York: St. Martin's, 1997.

The Guide to Classic Recorded Jazz. University of Iowa Press, 1995.

Setting the Tempo: Fifty Years of Great Jazz Liner Notes. New York: Doubleday, 1996.

Piazza, who has written about music for periodicals ranging from the *New York Times* to the *Oxford American,* is a trustworthy and opinionated guide to the music.

Rose, Al. *I Remember Jazz*. Baton Rouge: Louisiana State University Press, 1997.

Storyville. University of Alabama Press, 1974 paperback.

Two classics by one of the deans of New Orleans music history.

Scherman, Tony. *Backbeat: Earl Palmer's Story*. Washington, D.C.: Smithsonian Institution Press, 1999.

An as-told-to autobiography of the great New Orleans drummer who was co-creator of such hits as Little Richard's "Tutti Frutti" and Fats Domino's "I'm Walkin'."

Smith, Michael P. *A Joyful Noise: A Celebration of New Orleans Music*. Dallas: Taylor, 1990.

Mardi Gras Indians. Gretna, La.: Pelican, 1994.

New Orleans Jazzfest: A Pictorial History. Gretna, La.: Pelican, 1991.

Smith is a native New Orleanian who has been photographing New Orleans culture and music for decades. These books collect his work in three specific areas.

Starr, S. Frederick. *Bamboula! The Life and Times of Louis Moreau Gottschalk*. New York: Oxford University Press, 1995.

Biography of the New Orleans–born musician who was America's first internationally recognized composer.

Tisserand, Michael. *The Kingdom of Zydeco.* New York: Arcade, 1998.

Tisserand, editor of the weekly newspaper *Gambit,* is also one of the best writers on New Orleans music. This is his definitive history of that unique and festive music, zydeco, with a distinctive accordion sound and infectious rhythm created by rub-board players. This is also a book about the black Creole culture of south Louisiana. You'll meet many unforgettable characters along the way. From Clifton Chenier to Buckwheat Zydeco and Beau Jocque, Tisserand gives us a grand tour of the zydeco prairie. A final chapter, "Keys to the Kingdom," describes where to hear zydeco music—put your dancing shoes on.

FOLKLORE AND CARNIVAL

Ancelet, Barry Jean. *Cajun and Creole Folktales: The French Oral Tradition in South Louisiana.* Jackson: University Press of Mississippi, 1994 (paperback).
Ancelet, Barry Jean, Jay D. Edwards, and Glen Pitre. *Cajun Country.* Jackson: University Press of Mississippi, 1991.

These two books are important works about Cajun culture.

Berry, Jason. *The Spirit of Black Hawk: A Mystery of Africans and Indians.* Jackson: University Press of Mississippi, 1995.

A study of the origins of the traditions of spiritual churches in New Orleans.

Flake, Carol. *New Orleans: Behind the Masks of America's Most Exotic City.* New York: Grove, 1994.

This is one of the best Mardi Gras books ever written. Flake came to New Orleans to capture Carnival of 1992, when the institution was threatened by an antidiscrimination ordinance (many Carnival krewes are all-white and all-male private clubs). Flake captures the broad and elusive range of the celebration, and what it means to the old-line New Orleanian as well as the casual participant.

Gill, James. *Lords of Misrule: Mardi Gras and the Politics of Race in New Orleans.* Jackson: University Press of Mississippi, 1997.

Gill, an editorial columnist for the *Times-Picayune,* here explores the tangled roots of racial unrest and Carnival.

Hearn, Lafcadio. *"Gumbo Zhebes": A Little Dictionary of Creole Proverbs.* New Orleans: Temperance Hall Press, 1991.

A reissue of the 1885 edition of Hearn's collected proverbs.

Hurston, Zora Neale. *Mules and Men.* Available in many editions. Folklore collection.

Kinser, Samuel. *Carnival American Style: Mardi Gras at New Orleans and Mobile.* Chicago: University of Chicago Press, 1990.

A study of Carnival that is fascinating and provocative. Kinser visited New Orleans only twice in the writing of this book, and he seems to me to be a bit stronger on Carnival theory than actual practice.

Lindahl, Carl, and Carolyn Ware. *Cajun Mardi Gras Masks.* Jackson: University Press of Mississippi, 1990.

The first study of this folk art form.

Lindahl, Carl, Maida Owens, and C. Renee Harvison, eds. *Swapping Stories.* Jackson: University Press of Mississippi, 1997.

A wonderful anthology of Louisiana stories and storytellers.

Mitchell, Reid. *All on a Mardi Gras Day: Episodes in the History of New Orleans Carnival.* Cambridge: Harvard University Press, 1995.

Former New Orleanian Mitchell recounts in brief and accessible essays the diverse history and culture of Carnival.

Saxon, Lyle, ed. *Fabulous New Orleans.* New York: Appleton-Century, 1928.

Gumbo Ya-Ya: The Folklore of Louisiana. Boston: Houghton Mifflin, 1945.

Two of the classic works that came out of the WPA writers' project in New Orleans, which Saxon directed. *Fabulous New Orleans* contains some of the best writing on the city ever, and *Gumbo Ya-Ya* is the basic text for Louisiana folklore.

Henri Schindler. *Mardi Gras New Orleans*. Paris: Flammarion, 1997. This fabulous book by a contemporary Carnival designer describes the golden age of Carnival, from the 1850s to the 1950s, and provides an overview of the celebration's history, along with many beautiful reproductions of Carnival art, memorabilia, and photographs.

Smith, Michael P. *Mardi Gras Indians*. Gretna, La.: Pelican, 1994.
Spirit World: Pattern in the Expressive Folk Culture of Afro-American New Orleans. New Orleans: New Orleans Urban Folklife Society, 1984.
Smith documents in words and images two important cultural traditions—the spiritual churches and the Mardi Gras Indians, "tribes" of African Americans who dress in elaborate "Indian" costumes and parade on Mardi Gras and St. Joseph's Day.

Tallant, Robert. *Mardi Gras As It Was*. Garden City, N.Y.: Doubleday, 1948.
Voodoo in New Orleans. New York: Macmillan, 1946.
The Voodoo Queen. New York: Putnam, 1956.
Three classics by one of the great chroniclers of New Orleans.

Tassin, Myron. *Mardi Gras and Bacchus: Something Old, Something New*. Gretna, La.: Pelican, 1984.
A history of the Krewe of Bacchus.

Teish, Luisah. *Jambalaya: The Natural Woman's Book of Personal Charms and Practical Rituals*. New York: HarperCollins, 1988 paperback.
Carnival of the Spirit: Seasonal Celebrations and Rites of Passage. HarperSan Francisco, 1994.
A New Orleans native, Teish is a storyteller, priestess of Oshun (a Yoruba religion), and spiritual teacher.

New Orleans is a sensual, sybaritic city, and it is for her pleasures that she has long been celebrated. Mardi Gras is her day of days. . . . The observance of Mardi Gras predates all else, embracing and infusing all that followed—the colonial orphan's longing for the crown, the perpetual calendar of fantasy (of preparation, enactment, and of memory), the passions for music and dance—all have been played out amid New Orleans' extravagant vegetation, beneath her blazing suns and warlock moons. It is impossible to capture even one Mardi Gras in words or pictures; a population devoted to joy is not wont to leave records, and those created have had to endure a tropical climate notoriously unkind to paper and velvets.

—Henri Schindler, *Mardi Gras New Orleans*

Touchet, Leo, photographer, text by Vernel Bagneris, introduction by Ellis Marsalis Jr. *Rejoice When You Die: The New Orleans Jazz Funerals*. Baton Rouge: Louisiana State University Press, 1998.
Touchet's gorgeous black-and-white photographs capture New Orleans jazz funerals in the 1960s and 1970s, with an impressionistic text by actor/playwright Vernel Bagneris *(One Mo' Time)*. Marsalis's introduction gives a good overview of jazz funeral customs. There is an accompanying CD of the same title, featuring traditional jazz funeral favorites by the DeJan Brass Band.

POETRY

Rather than attempt to describe the work of these poets individually, we have simply listed some of the books by noted poets with New Orleans connections.

ANTHOLOGIES

Bonner, Thomas Jr., and Robert E. Skinner. *Immortelles: Poems of Life and Death by New Southern Writers*. New Orleans: Xavier Review Press, 1995.
Includes work by forty southern poets.

Codrescu, Andrei, and Laura Rosenthal, eds. *American Poets Say Goodbye to the Twentieth Century*. New York: Four Walls, Eight Windows, 1996.
―――. *Up Late: American Poetry since 1970*. New York: Four Walls, Eight Windows. 1990.
Terrific anthologies of contemporary poetry, with many New Orleans poets represented.

Dobie, Ann Brewster. *Uncommonplace: An Anthology of Contemporary Louisiana Poets*. Baton Rouge: Louisiana State University Press, 1998.
This anthology features the work of sixty-seven Louisiana writers.

Salaam, Kalamu ya. *From a Bend in the River: 100 New Orleans Poets*. New Orleans: Runagate Press, 1998.

Originally begun as a project at the Contemporary Arts Center in 1990, this anthology includes work that displays the vitality and diversity of New Orleans poets—male and female, young and old, gay and straight, black and white.

Travis, John, ed. *The Maple Leaf Rag: 15th Anniversary Anthology.* New Orleans: Portals Press, 1994.
Celebrates fifteen years of the Maple Leaf Bar reading series and includes work by many of the poets who have read there over the years.

INDIVIDUAL WORKS

Adamo, Ralph. *End of the World.* Fayetteville, Ark.: Lost Roads. 1979.
Hanoi Rose. New Orleans: New Orleans Poetry Journal Press, 1989.
Sadness at the Private University. Fayetteville, Ark.: Lost Roads, 1978.

Brosman, Catharine Savage. *Journeying from Canyon de Chelly.* Baton Rouge: Louisiana State University Press, 1990.

Cassin, Maxine. *Turnip's Blood.* Baton Rouge: Sisters Grim Press, 1985.

Codrescu, Andrei. *Alien Candor: Selected Poems, 1970–1995.* Santa Rosa, Calif.: Black Sparrow, 1996.

Cooley, Nicole. *Resurrection.* Baton Rouge: Louisiana State University Press, 1996.

Cooley, Peter. *The Astonished Hours.* Pittsburgh: Carnegie-Mellon, 1992.
The Company of Strangers. Pittsburgh: Carnegie-Mellon, 1992.
Nightseasons. Pittsburgh: Carnegie-Mellon, 1983.

The Room Where Summer Ends. Pittsburgh: Carnegie-Mellon, 1979.
Sacred Conversations. Pittsburgh: Carnegie-Mellon, 1997.

Dent, Tom. *Blue Lights and River Songs.* Detroit: Lotus, 1982.

Grue, Lee Meitzen. *In the Sweet Balance of the Flesh.* Austin: Plain View Press, 1996.

Harris, Nancy. *The Ape Woman Story.* Paradis, La.: Pirogue, 1989.

Kamenetz, Rodger. *The Missing Jew.* St. Louis, Mo.: Time Being Books, 1992.

Kane, Julie. *Body and Soul.* New Orleans: Pirogue, 1987.

Katrovas, Richard. *Book of Complaints.* Pittsburgh: Carnegie-Mellon, 1993.
Green Dragons. Middletown, Conn.: Wesleyan University Press, 1983.
Prague, U.S.A. New Orleans: Portals Press, 1996.
The Public Mirror. Middletown, Conn.: Wesleyan University Press, 1990.
Snug Harbor. Middletown, Conn.: Wesleyan University Press, 1986.

Komunyakaa, Yusef. *Neon Vernacular: New and Selected Poems.* Hanover, N.H.: Wesleyan University Press/University Press of New England, 1993.
Winner of the 1994 Pulitzer Prize for poetry.

Maddox, Everette. *American Waste.* New Orleans: Portals Press, 1993.
Bar Scotch. Paradis, La.: Pirogue, 1988.
The Everette Maddox Songbook. New Orleans Poetry Journal Press, 1982.

Murphy, Kay. *Belief Blues.* New Orleans: Portals Press, 1998.

Osbey, Brenda Marie. *All Saints.* Baton Rouge: Louisiana State University Press, 1997.
Winner of the 1998 American Book Award.
Ceremony for Minneconjoux. Lexington, Ky.: Callaloo Poetry Series, 1983.
Desperate Circumstance, Dangerous Woman. Brownsville, Ore.: Story Line Press, 1991.
In These Houses. Middletown, Conn.: Wesleyan University Press, 1988.

Rice, Stan. *Fear Itself.* New York: Alfred A. Knopf, 1995.
Radiance of Pigs. New York, Alfred A. Knopf, 1999.
Singing Yet: New and Selected Poems. New York: Alfred A. Knopf, 1992.

CHILDREN'S BOOKS

Amoss, Berthe. *Cajun Gingerbread Boy.* New York: Hyperion, 1995.
Chalk Cross. New York: Seabury Press, 1976.
Lost Magic. New York: Hyperion, 1993.
Mockingbird Song. New York: Harper & Row, 1988.
Artist and illustrator Amoss has created a local classic in retelling the story of the gingerbread man with a Cajun twist. *Chalk Cross* is a novel for young readers about Marie Laveau, *Lost Magic* is set in the Middle Ages, and *Mockingbird Song* is about a young girl growing up in New Orleans.

Coles, Robert, illustrated by George Ford. *The Story of Ruby Bridges.* New York: Scholastic, 1995.
Psychiatrist Robert Coles has retold the life story of Ruby Bridges, one of the four young girls who integrated the New Orleans public schools.

Dartez, Cecilia Casrill. *Jenny Giraffe and the Streetcar Party.* Gretna, La.: Pelican, 1993.

Jenny Giraffe Discovers Papa Noel. Gretna, La.: Pelican, 1994.
Jenny Giraffe Discovers the French Quarter. Gretna, La.: Pelican, 1992.
Jenny Giraffe's Mardi Gras Ride. Gretna, La.: Pelican, 1997.
L Is for Louisiana. Stillwater, Minn.: Voyageur, 1993.
Jenny Giraffe is a goofy, endearing creature who explores life in New Orleans very much from a child's point of view. *L Is for Louisiana* is a photographic alphabet of the state.

Doucet, Sharon. *Why Lapin's Ears Are Long and Other Tales from Louisiana.* New York: Orchard Books, 1997.
Doucet lives in Cajun country; her husband is Cajun musician Michael Doucet of the popular band Beausoleil. This selection of folk tales has charming illustrations.

Fontenot, Mary Alice. Clovis Crawfish series. More than fifteen volumes in this series, published by Pelican.
Mardi Gras in the Country. Gretna, La: Pelican, 1994.
Fontenot's Clovis Crawfish books, which tell stories of the lives of a crawfish and the swamp creatures who are his friends, with such engaging titles as *Clovis Crawfish and Batiste Bête Puante* (a skunk) or *Clovis Crawfish and Etienne Escargot,* are popular with children all over the world. There are pronunciation guides in the back, so you can work on your Cajun accent.

Holt, Kimberly Willis. *My Louisiana Sky.* New York: Henry Holt, 1998.
This young-adult novel by a Louisiana native, telling a young girl's coming-of-age story, is set in a small central Louisiana town in the 1950s.

Lockwood, C. C. *C. C. Lockwood's Louisiana Nature Guide.* Baton Rouge: Louisiana State University Press, 1995.
Nature photographer Lockwood explores the natural world of the state, along with lots of suggestions for activities outdoors.

McConduit, Denise Walter. *D.J. and the Zulu Parade.* Gretna, La.: Pelican, 1994.

D.J. Goes to Jazz Fest. Gretna, La.: Pelican, 1997.
D.J. is a young African American boy exploring New Orleans festivals and traditions.

Renaux. J. J. *Why Alligator Hates Dog.* Little Rock: August House, 1995.
Hilarious folktale, fun to read aloud.

Shaik, Fatima. *The Jazz of Our Street.* New York: Dial Books for Young Readers, 1997.
Melitte. New York: Dial Books for Young Readers, 1997.
On Mardi Gras Day. New York: Dial Books for Young Readers, 1998.
Shaik, a New Orleans native, explores the heritage of the city in two picture books; *Melitte* is a young adult novel which explores the institution of slavery through the eyes of a young slave girl.

Soper, Celia, author, Patrick Soper, illustrator. *Cajun Folktales.* Gretna, La.: Pelican, 1997.
More Cajun folktales.

Thomassie, Tynia. *Feliciana Feydra LeRoux: A Cajun Tall Tale.* Illustrated by Cat Bowman. Boston: Little, Brown, 1995.
A wonderful picture book about a little girl who wants to go on an alligator hunt, even though she's left behind because she's a girl. A wonderful story of bravery and determination, and lots of fun to read aloud.

Van Laan, Nancy. *With a Whoop and a Holler: A Bushel of Lore from Way Down South.* Illustrated by Scott Cook. New York: Atheneum Books for Young Readers, 1998.
Van Laan, a Baton Rouge native, includes a wonderful selection of Louisiana stories drawn from such sources as Alcée Fortier's *Memoirs of the American Folklore Society,* Lafcadio Hearn's *"Gombo Zhebes,"* and Joel Chandler Harris's *Nights with Uncle Remus.* The lively, antic illustrations bring the story alive for young readers as well as adult lovers of folklore.

COOKBOOKS

Austin, Leslie. *Chez Helene Cookbook*. New Orleans: De Simonin Publishing, 1984.

Bienvenu, Marcelle. *Who's Your Mama, Are You Catholic, and Can You Make a Roux?* Lafayette, La.: Times of Acadiana Press, 1991, revised in 1992 and 1996.

Brennan, Ella, and Dick Brennan. *Commander's Palace Cookbook*. New York: Clarkson N. Potter, 1984.

Brennan, Pip, Jimmy Brennan, and Ted Brennan. *Breakfast at Brennan's and Dinner Too*. New Orleans: Brennan's, 1994.

Brennan's Restaurant. *Brennan's New Orleans Cookbook*. New Orleans: R. L. Crager, 1961.

Chase, Leah. *The Dooky Chase Cookbook*. Gretna, La.: Pelican, 1990.

Collin, Rima, and Richard Collin. *The New Orleans Cookbook: Creole, Cajun, and Louisiana French Recipes Past and Present*. New York, Knopf, 1975.
    Still the best basic sampler of New Orleans cooking.

Folse, John. *Chef John Folse's Louisiana Sampler: Recipes from Our Fairs and Festivals*. Gonzales, La.: Chef John Folse & Co., 1994.
————. *Chef John Folse's Plantation Celebrations: Recipes from Our Louisiana Mansions*. Gonzales, La.: Chef John Folse & Co., 1994.
Folse, John, and Craig M. Walker. *Something Old, Something New: Louisiana Cooking with a Change of Heart*. Gonzales, La.: Chef John Folse & Co., 1997.

Galatoire, Leon. *Leon Galatoire's Cookbook*. Gretna, La.: Pelican, 1994.

Graham, Kevin. *Simply Elegant: The Cuisine of the Windsor Court Hotel.* New York: Grove Weidenfeld, 1991.

Guste, Roy F. *Antoine's Restaurant Cookbook.* New Orleans: Carbery-Guste, 1978.

Hearn, Lafcadio. *Lafcadio Hearn's Creole Cook Book.* Gretna, La.: Pelican, 1990.
  For literary history buffs. First published in 1885 as *La Cuisine Creole.*

Hellman, Lillian, and Peter Feibleman. *Eating Together: Recollections and Recipes.* Boston: Little, Brown, 1984.
  The two share memories of living and cooking together over their long friendship in New Orleans and on Martha's Vineyard, including their competing recipes for gumbo.

Junior League of Baton Rouge. *River Road Recipes.* Baton Rouge: Junior League of Baton Rouge, 1959.
  The original, which has been followed by *River Road Recipes II* and *River Road Recipes III.*

Junior League of New Orleans. *The Plantation Cookbook.* Garden City, N.Y.: Doubleday, 1972 (reprint New Orleans: B. E. Trice, 1992).

Lagasse, Emeril, with Jessie Tirsch. *Emeril's New Orleans Cooking.* New York, William Morrow, 1993.
Lagasse, Emeril, with Marcelle Bienvenu. *Emeril's Creole Christmas.* New York: William Morrow, 1997.
———. *Louisiana Real and Rustic.* New York: William Morrow, 1997.

New Orleans Museum of Art, Women's Volunteer Committee. *The Artist's Palate Cookbook Classic Creole and New Orleans Recipes.* New Orleans: New Orleans Museum of Art, 1986.

Patout, Alex. *Patout's Cajun Home Cooking.* New York: Random House, 1986.

Preuss, Gunter, and Evelyn Preuss. *Broussard's Restaurant Cookbook*. Gretna, La.: Pelican, 1996.

Prudhomme, Paul. *Chef Paul Prudhomme's Louisiana Kitchen*. New York: William Morrow, 1984.
————. *Prudhomme Family Cookbook*. New York: William Morrow, 1987.

Stewart, Richard. *Gumbo Shop: Traditional and Contemporary Creole Cuisine*. New Orleans: Gumbo Shop, 1999.

Theriot, Jude W. *La Meilleure de la Louisiane*. Lake Charles, La.: J. W. Theriot, 1980.

Times-Picayune. *The Picayune Cookbook*. 1901; revised by Marcelle Bienvenu and reissued by Random House in a sesquicentennial edition in 1987.

Delos Smith doesn't agree with me about New Orleans. He wouldn't. He's too self-conscious himself and besides that he's an immigrant and a sentimentalist. The thing I talk about is not apparent on the surface. It is millions of miles deep. You feel it more than you see it. And if you hadn't lived here all your life you wouldn't even feel it. Anyway, if you ever think of coming back, come back soon. It won't be the same place in ten years. Take my word for it.

John McClure and I talked for a long time last night. We talked about a great many things but mostly about how disgusted we were with literature. There is a good reason for our disgust. Everybody we know talks about literature. Even the waiters in Gluck's talk about literature. I went to see a reporter who works on the paper who was arrested and put in jail for embezzling $176,000 from a Los Angeles bank two years ago and the first thing he did was to talk about literature. With murderers and thieves and dope-peddlers all around him, men waiting in cells to be hung, he started talking about literature. Jesus!

You know, when I think of a whole world going about with the smudge of typewriter ribbon on its fingers, I become so ashamed I want to go off somewhere and hide. I become ashamed of my own smudged fingers. I become ashamed of the book I have written and all the books I want to write. I become ashamed even of the thoughts I think. If I were half-way logical I should never write another line.

Take the crowd in the French Quarter for instance—the ones who sit around the book-shops and swap ideas. They make me feel as though I ought to hurry home and take a bath. Possibly there is some genuine work being done, some sincere emotion being felt, but if so I am sure it is being done and felt in an obscure garret that nobody knows about.

—Hamilton Basso, "New Orleans Letter,"

in *transition* (February 1929)

New Orleans Bookshops

NEW ORLEANS HAS a long history of independent and specialty book shops. Don't underestimate the bookseller's penchant for giving advice—on everything from the best new title to the best neighborhood restaurant. The New Orleans Gulf South Booksellers Association has created a map of independent bookstores, available at member stores. Some stores are open late or on Sundays; call for business hours. For more information about the New Orleans Gulf South Booksellers Association, write P.O. Box 750043, New Orleans, LA 70175-0043.

GENERAL BOOKSHOPS (INDEPENDENT)

Beaucoup Books
5414 Magazine St. (Uptown)
New Orleans, LA 70115
(504) 895-2663
1-800-543-4114
Owner: Mary Price Dunbar

This shop, founded in 1983, reflects the eclectic tastes of its owner (who is married to mystery novelist Tony Dunbar), with emphasis on fine fiction, local-interest titles, travel and foreign-language books, and children's books. Lots of wonderful postcards and greeting cards. Great neighborhood for browsing, with interesting shops all along Magazine St.

Beaucoup Books, Too
200 Broadway at the River (Uptown)
New Orleans, LA 70118
(504) 865-8310

Writers Tony Dunbar (left) and Richard Ford with bookseller
Mary Price Dunbar at Beaucoup Books

Photo by Earl Perry

Owner: Mary Price Dunbar
Manager: Carol Antosiak
This small, jewel-like shop in Uptown Square (it was formerly the
Uptown Square Book Shop) was founded in 1985 by bookseller
Mark Zumpe. Mary Price Dunbar purchased it in 1999 and estab-
lished specialties in regional and travel books. Settle in on the green
leather sofa for a read or a chat, or browse in nearby stores as well.

deVille Books & Prints
344 Carondelet (Central Business District)
New Orleans, LA 70130
(504) 525-1846
FAX (504) 525-5264
Owner: Julian Mutter
Manager: Dave Brewington

The store, named for the late New Orleans bookseller George deVille, was founded in 1977. It moved to this location, formerly a bank building, in 1994 (the previous location appeared in *The Vampire Lestat,* in which the title character steps into the bookshop to find a copy of *Interview with the Vampire*). The shop offers an interesting selection of new and used books, specializing in the South and Louisiana titles, and a large assortment of antiquarian prints of New Orleans and Louisiana, including maps and ephemera. Manager Dave Brewington is an accredited appraiser.

deVille Books & Prints
1 Poydras St.
#10 Riverwalk (on the Mississippi, next to the Convention Center)
New Orleans, LA 70130
(504) 595-8916

James Lee Burke (right) at the Garden District Book Shop
with owner Britton Trice

Photo by Earl Perry

Owner: Julian Mutter
Manager: Theresa Cuny
This branch of deVille Books carries local-interest books and prints—"fifty-eight shelves of local interest"—and caters to the tourist trade that frequents the popular Riverwalk shopping mall.

Garden District Book Shop
2727 Prytania in the Rink (Garden District)
New Orleans, LA 70130
(504) 895-2266
FAX (504) 895-0111
Owner: Britton Trice
Manager: Deb Wehmeier

There are frequent autographings in this shop, with its eclectic selection and strengths in gardening, interior design, and regional New Orleans titles. The store opened at this location—the building housed the ice-skating rink for the 1884 world's fair—in 1979, after three years on Jackson Ave. Stop in at the PJ's downstairs for coffee. Trice is also a publisher; he publishes Anne Rice's works in special limited editions, as well as the work of authors such as Richard Ford, James Lee Burke, Carl Hiaasen, and Cormac McCarthy. For information about the limited editions, write B. E. Trice Publishing at the same address.

Maple Street Book Shop
7523 Maple St.
New Orleans, 70118
(504) 866-4916
(504) 866-7059
Owner: Rhoda Faust

Founded in 1964, this shop in an old house in the University area is a local favorite. Owner Rhoda Faust has a long history in New Orleans bookselling, and visitors will admire the photographs of author appearances that adorn the walls. Helpful staff and good selection, with specialties in contemporary, classic, and mystery fiction, particularly local-interest titles and the work of Walker Percy, who was one of Faust's mentors. Faust, with her Faust Publishing

Company, published Linda Hobson's *Walker Percy: A Comprehensive Descriptive Bibliography,* and three works by Percy: *Diagnosing the Modern Malaise, Novel-Writing in an Apocalyptic Time,* and *State of the Novel.* Staff favorites are always a good bet, and there is a fine selection of nonfiction as well.

Maple Street Old Metairie Book Shop
200 Metairie Rd. (Old Metairie)
Metairie, LA 70005
(504) 832-8937
Owners: Rhoda Faust and Britton Trice
Manager: Jamie Ramoneda

This branch of the Maple Street Book Shops is ensconced in a modern specialty shopping center in old Metairie. Manager Jamie Ramoneda maintains a good general bookstore with a diverse selection, personally choosing every title; she has strong specialties in literary fiction and travel. Nice browsing in the other stores in the center, and a nearby coffee shop.

SPECIALTY SHOPS

African American Bookshops

Afro-American Book Stop—two locations
The Plaza Shopping Center (New Orleans East)
5700 Read Blvd. #275
New Orleans, LA 70127
(504) 243-2436
FAX (504) 243-2255

New Orleans Center (Central Business District)
1400 Poydras St.
New Orleans, LA 70112
(504) 588-1474
Owner: Michele Lewis (Lewis also manages the Plaza location)
Manager, New Orleans Center store: Bunny Lewis

These stores cater to the local community with Afro-American cards, books by and about African Americans, games, puzzles for children, and Kwanzaa supplies. Most leading African American authors visit this store or the Community Book Center on their New Orleans tours. Michele Lewis was named Blackboard's bookseller of the year for 1998.

Community Book Center
219 N. Broad St. (Central City)
New Orleans, LA 70119
(504) 822-BOOK or 822-2665
Owner: Vera Warren-Williams
Manager: Jennifer Turner

The oldest African American bookstore in New Orleans, Community Book Center offers a good selection of African American books, and carries cards, books, games, puzzles, Kwanzaa supplies, and a strong Christian section with church supplies. The store is also a good source of information about community events.

Art Books

A Gallery for Fine Photography
322 Royal St. (French Quarter)
New Orleans, LA 70130
(504) 568-1313
Owner: Josh Pailet

Known for its impressive selection of photographic prints, covering luminaries from Cartier-Bresson to Robert Mapplethorpe, along with locals such as George Dureau and Josephine Sacabo. Pailet (himself the author of a photographic work on New Orleans's 1984 World's Fair) augments the art with the city's best collection of new and used books on photography. There are rare photographs and books from the nineteenth as well as the twentieth century. The warm, charming French Quarter interior is inviting, and there are frequent appearances and book signings by photographers.

New Orleans Museum of Art Book Shop
New Orleans Museum of Art

City Park
New Orleans, LA 70179
(504) 488-2631
FAX (504) 484-6662
Manager: Eleanor Meade
The best selection of art books in the city, as well as gifts, posters, and exhibition catalogs, with a specialty in children's art books.

Children's Books

Maple Street Children's Book Shop
7529 Maple (Uptown)
New Orleans, LA 70118
(504) 861-2105
Owners: Rhoda Faust and Cindy Dike
This charming shop in another old house next to the Maple Street Book Shop proper might look familiar: it once appeared in a national commercial for VISA. Cindy Dike has assembled a strong collection of books for children up to age fourteen, as well as books on pregnancy, child care, and education. There's usually a story hour Saturday at 1 P.M. The store was founded in 1973.

Gay and Lesbian Books

Faubourg Marigny Bookstore
600 Frenchmen (Faubourg Marigny)
New Orleans, LA 70116
(504) 943-9875
Owner: Alan Robinson
Specializing in gay and lesbian literature, FM Books, founded in 1978, is one of the oldest gay bookstores in the country. The store holds frequent signings and carries periodicals, CDs, and gift items in addition to an excellent selection of books. It is also a good source of local information about the gay and lesbian community. It stays open late to capitalize on the lively foot traffic in this interesting neighborhood—check out the action at the Praline Connection restaurant and the Café Brasil across the street. Several

good music venues, including Snug Harbor and the Dream Palace, are in the neighborhood.

Louisiana Specialties

The Historic New Orleans Collection
531 Royal St. (French Quarter)
New Orleans, LA 70130
(504) 598-7147
FAX (504) 897-7108
Manager: Sue Laudeman

Large selection of books on Louisiana history and culture, architecture, the Civil War; first editions; and an unusual selection of gift items, particularly antique jewelry, vintage prints and silver, and reproductions from the Collection.

The Louisiana Catalog Store
14839 W. Main St.
Cut Off, LA 70345
(504) 632-4100

Run by filmmaker Glen Pitre and his wife, Michelle Benoit, this is a retail store as well as a mail-order operation specializing in Louisiana books, music, and gift items.

Metaphysical Bookstores

Golden Leaves Centre
3242 Severn Ave. (Metairie)
Metairie, LA 7011
(504) 888-5208
Owner: Lawrence Fothe

Metaphysical and new age books and services.

Life's Journey Bookstore
3313 Richland Ave. (Metairie)
Metairie, LA 70002
(504) 885-2375

Owner: Beatrice Scaffiti
Metaphysical and new age books and services.

Religious Bookstores

Baptist Bookstore
3939 Gentilly Blvd. (Gentilly)
New Orleans, LA 70126
(504) 282-2626
Manager: Barry Anderson
This large store on the campus of the New Orleans Baptist Theological Seminary is open to the public. It carries Bibles, devotional texts, hymnals, music, and more.

Catholic Book Store
8039 Fig St. (Carrollton)
New Orleans, LA
(504) 861-7504
Manager: Anne Wall
More than fifty years old, this is a fully stocked store for Catholic readers, with books, Bibles, music, and religious articles. It serves as the bookstore for the adjacent seminary but appeals to the layperson as well.

Good News Book Store
201 Schlief
Belle Chasse, LA 70037
Owners: Peetsie Cummings and Ray Cummings
(504) 394-3087
Bibles, Christian books, music, and gifts.

Letters & Etc.
1525 Lapalco Blvd. Unit 9
Harvey, LA 70058
(504) 366-8104
Owner: Karen Trudeaux
Christian books and gifts.

Superlative Expressions
5703 Read Blvd, Suite F
New Orleans, LA
(504) 242-8555
Owner: Joyce Richmond and Joan Reeves
Bibles, books, and Christian gifts.

Used and Antiquarian Bookshops

Arcadian Books
714 Orleans Ave. (French Quarter)
(504) 523-4138
Owner: Russell Desmond
This store, in business since 1981, has a good general selection supplemented with French-language items and current material on Louisiana history, as well as a nice choice of out-of-print books. This a bookshop for Francophiles and would be a memorable stop for French tourists. Desmond is extremely knowledgeable and highly opinionated about Louisiana literature and history.

Beckham's Book Shop
228 Decatur St. (French Quarter)
New Orleans, LA 70130
(504) 522-9875
Owners: Carey Beckham and Alton Cook
You can spend all day in this two-story shop, with one of the finest selection of used books in the city. The store, in this location since 1970, also has a specialty in classical music on records and CDs, as well as sheet music. Open seven days a week.

The Book Rack
2305 Metairie Rd.
Metairie, LA
(504) 834-7569
Owner: Phyllis Feran
Trades and sells paperbacks. Large selection. Open seven days a week.

Crescent City Books
204 Chartres (French Quarter)
New Orleans, LA 70130
(504) 524-4997
Manager: Dan Cwik

A two-story, scholarly, used and antiquarian bookstore specializing in world history and art. Search service and cataloger. Open seven days a week.

Dauphine Street Books
410 Dauphine St. (French Quarter)
New Orleans, LA 70112
(504) 529-2333
Owner: Steve Lacy

This shop specializes in modern literature, art and photography, local history, and jazz history. (The building was the first elegant parlor house of legendary madam Norma Wallace, the subject of a recent biography by Christine Wiltz.)

Faulkner House Books
624 Pirate's Alley (French Quarter)
New Orleans, LA 70116
(504) 524-2940
Owners: Joseph DeSalvo Jr. ad Rosemary James

This small, elegant shop specializing in fine southern literature in rare and first editions is on the ground floor of a building where Faulkner lived while in New Orleans. Right off Jackson Square, facing St. Anthony's garden, it's the perfect place to while away an afternoon.

George Herget Books
3109 Magazine St. (Uptown)
New Orleans, LA 70115
(504) 891-5595
Owner: Jean Nosich

Named for its late owner, a beloved New Orleans bookseller who passed it on to a longtime employee, this shop is one of the great treasures of Uptown. Smell the books, look at the postcards and sheet music, and sit a spell. The store specializes in regional books, including Civil War and other historical titles, cookbooks, and art books. A great place to watch the Irish Channel St. Patrick's Day parade.

Great Acquisitions Book Service
8200 Hampson St. (Uptown)
New Orleans, LA 70118
(504) 861-8707
Owner: Joseph Cohen

Begun as a retirement occupation for its owner, a former Tulane University professor, Great Acquisitions rapidly expanded to a full-time occupation. Browse through Joseph Cohen's fine selection of works on Louisiana, the South, general Americana, art, literature, and history, or get him to do a search for titles you want.

Kaboom Books
915 Barracks St. (French Quarter)
New Orleans, LA 70116
(504) 529-5780
Owners: John and Dee Dillman

One of the most intriguing shops in the Quarter, with good, reasonably priced books and a large selection. Open seven days a week. This bookstore inspired the fictional French Quarter store BOOKS in Louis Edwards's novel *N: A Romantic Mystery*. No junk, no air conditioning.

Librairie Book Shop
823 Chartres (French Quarter)
New Orleans, LA 70116
(504) 525-4837
FAX (504) 821-6670
Owner: Carey Beckham

The light from Librairie, another of Carey Beckham's shops, casts a warm glow over the Quarter. Stop by in the evening. In business since 1967, the shop features antiquarian books, postcards, and old prints.

McLaughlin Books
512 Terry Parkway
Terrytown, LA
(504) 367-3754
Owner: Mary McLaughlin
Used paperbacks and hardbacks. Open since 1978. Open seven days.

Paperback Palace
6309 Airline Highway
New Orleans, LA
(504) 733-7261
Manager: Elizabeth DeLaughter
Trades and sells used paperbacks. Open seven days.

University Bookstores

Loyola University Bookstore
Loyola University
Danna Center
New Orleans, LA 70118
(504) 865-3262

University of New Orleans Bookstore
University Center
New Orleans, LA 70148
(504) 280-6373

Tulane University Bookstore
University Center
New Orleans, LA 70118
(504) 865-5913

CHAIN STORES

B. Dalton
714 Canal St.

New Orleans, LA 70130
(504) 529-2705

B. Dalton/Lakeside Mall
3301 Veterans Hwy.
Metairie, LA 70002
(504) 837-2868
Manager: John Lambrecht

B. Dalton/Oakwood Mall
197-56 Westbank Expressway
Gretna, LA 70053
(504) 362-2074

Barnes & Noble Booksellers
3721 Veterans Memorial Blvd.
Metairie, LA 70002
(504) 455-4929
Manager: Michael Villescaz
Community Relations Manager: Phone (504) 455-5135

Books-A-Million/Gretna
197B Westbank Expressway
Gretna, LA 70053
(504) 364-1070

Bookstar (A Barnes & Noble store)
Jax Brewery Marketplace
414 N. Peters
New Orleans, LA 70130
(504) 523-6411

Borders Books Music Video & Café
3131 Veterans Memorial Blvd.
Metairie, LA 70002
(504) 835-1363
Manager: Jeremy Reed

Community Relations Coordinator: Melissa Grantadam (504) 835-9176

Waldenbooks/Clearview
4420 Veterans Blvd.
Clearview Shopping Center
Metairie, LA 70006
(504) 888-1275
Manager: Mike Murphy

Waldenbooks/Lakeside
3301 Veterans Blvd.
Lakeside Mall
Metairie, LA 70002
(504) 834-8455

Waldenbooks/New Orleans Center
New Orleans Center
1400 Poydras
New Orleans, LA 70112
(504) 525-8211

BOOKS ON TAPE

Bestseller Audio
3501 Severn Ave. (Metairie)
Suite 3-C
Metairie, LA 70002
(504) 455-0590

and

1597 Gause Blvd. (Slidell)
Slidell, LA 70458
(504) 847-2834
Owner: Ric Smith

These stores are devoted entirely to books on tape and CD, for sale or rent. Open seven days a week.

OTHER BOOK SERVICES

Appraiser

Dave Brewington
c/o deVille Books and Prints
344 Carondelet St.
New Orleans, LA 70130
(504) 525-1846
Member of the Appraisers Association of America.

Book Wholesaler

Forest Sales & Distributing Company
4157 St. Louis St.
New Orleans, LA 70119
(504) 947-2106
Louisiana: 1-800-349-2106
Other U.S.: 1-800-347-2106
Owner: Joseph Arrigo
This wholesale distributor of regional-interest books and cookbooks has served the region since 1967.

Beneath the immaculate shapes of lamps we passed, between ancient softly greenish gates, and here was Jackson park. Sparrows were upon Andrew Jackson's head as, childishly conceived, he bestrode his curly horse in terrific arrested motion. Beneath his remote stare people gaped and a voice was saying: "Greatest piece of statuary in the world: made entirely of bronze, weighing two and a half tons, and balanced on its hind feet." And thinking of how our great men have suffered at the hands of the municipal governments which they strove to make possible, pondering on how green the trees were, and the grass, and the narcissi and hyacinths like poised dancers; blessing that genius who conceived a park without any forbidden signs, where tramps could lie in the sun and children and dogs could pleasure themselves in the grass without reprimand; I remarked to Spratling how no one since Cezanne had really dipped his brush in light. Spratling, whose hand has been shaped to a brush as mine has (alas!) not, here became discursive on the subject of transferring light to canvas; but not listening to him I looked at the faces of old men sitting patiently on iron benches as we slowly paced— men who had learned that living is not only not passionate or joyous, but not even especially sorrowful.

—William Faulkner, "Out of Nazareth,"
in *New Orleans Sketches*

What's Happening through the Year: A Literary Calendar

THE TENNESSEE WILLIAMS/NEW ORLEANS LITERARY FESTIVAL

THE TENNESSEE WILLIAMS/New Orleans Literary Festival celebrates the literary heritage of the city in the name of its best-known former literary resident. From its founding in the spring of 1987, this grassroots community festival has grown into a national literary event that attracts an audience of several thousand.

The festival usually takes place during the weekend in March closest to the playwright's birthday (March 26) and is headquartered at Le Petit Theatre, 616 St. Peter in the French Quarter. A Tennessee Williams play usually serves as the festival's centerpiece; other activities include literary panels and readings, addresses by noted writers, a book fair, literary walking tours, and several parties. All events are by admission. Past festivals have featured such authors as Robert Olen Butler, Richard Ford, Ernest Gaines, and Anne Rice and such theater personalities as Elizabeth Ashley, Alec Baldwin, Anne Jackson, and Eli Wallach. Cassette tapes of festival panels are available.

The festival includes the French Quarter Literary Conference, a series of master classes with authors, poets, journalists, agents, and other literary professionals. The Tennessee Williams Scholars' Conference brings together academic specialists in the playwright's life and work, and sponsors a publication, the *Tennessee Williams Annual Review*.

For more information, write the Tennessee Williams/New Orleans Literary Festival, 5500 Prytania St., Suite 217, New Orleans, LA 70115 or call (504) 581-1144 or visit the festival's Web site at www.gnofn.org/~twfest.

Stella and Stanley Shouting Contest,
1998 Tennessee Williams/New Orleans Literary Festival

Photo by Michael DeMocker

THE SYMPHONY BOOK FAIR

The city's largest book fair benefits the Louisiana Philharmonic Orchestra and is held each April at the University of New Orleans

Lakefront Arena. The sale includes art, sheet music, records and CDs, and some very rare books. The fair accepts donations all year round. Call (504) 861-2004 for dates and specifics.

FRIENDS FEST

A May tradition, this weekend festival is sponsored by the Friends of the New Orleans Public Library. Held on the grounds of the beautiful Latter Library on St. Charles Ave., the fest centers on a book sale, with lots of children's activities and a patrons' party. For information, write the Friends of the New Orleans Public Library, 219 Loyola Ave., New Orleans 70112 or call (504) 596-2587 for more information.

JAZZFEST BOOK TENT

The world-renowned New Orleans Jazz and Heritage Festival, which vibrantly fills the last weekend of April and the first weekend in May, is a great feast of music and food. The New Orleans Gulf South Booksellers Association members band together to run a book tent that offers a broad selection of books about Louisiana music and culture. Proceeds go to the Children's Book Bank and to various literacy projects. Watch for celebrity autographings by such notables as Buddy Guy, Dr. John, and Wynton Marsalis. Information is available at independent bookstores in the area, through the Jazzfest office at (504) 941-5100, or on the Web site at www.nojazzfest.com.

THE ESSENCE MUSIC FESTIVAL

Billed as a "party with a purpose" and sponsored by *Essence* magazine during the July 4 holiday weekend, this music festival brings an all-star lineup of musical talent to the Superdome. But readers will also enjoy the Festival Market at the Ernest M. Morial Convention Center, also the scene of the Festival's Empowerment Seminars, which have featured such leading African American authors and motivational speakers as *Essence* editor Susan Taylor, Terry

McMillan, Randall Robinson, Bertice Berry, and Iyanla VanZant. Check *Essence* magazine or call 1-800-ESSENCE for information.

WORDS AND MUSIC: A LITERARY FEAST IN NEW ORLEANS

The Pirate's Alley Faulkner Society was founded by Joseph DeSalvo Jr. and Rosemary James, owners of Faulkner House Books, to "celebrate the written word." The society hosts a birthday bash every September on the weekend closest to William Faulkner's September 25 birthday. Admission is free with membership in the society, which is open to everyone. Tickets for the public begin at $50.

In 1997 the society added Words and Music: A Literary Feast in New Orleans, a writers' conference interspersed with musical performances, during the same weekend. There is an admission charge to these literary and musical events.

The society publishes a literary journal, the *Double Dealer Redux,* named after the original *Double Dealer* of the 1920s, and sponsors the William Faulkner Creative Writing Competition. There are six divisions—novels, novellas, short stories, personal essays, poetry, and high school short stories. Winners receive their awards (generous cash prizes and commemorative medals) at the Faulkner birthday celebration.

For more information, including guidelines and entry forms for the writing competition, write the society at 632 Pirate's Alley, New Orleans 70116-3254, call (504) 586-1612, or check out the Web site, http://members.aol.com/faulkhouse.

HALLOWEEN

The weekend closest to this holiday is traditionally devoted to celebrating the work of author Anne Rice. Usually she has a new novel out at that time, so there are book signings (she usually holds the first at the Garden District Book Shop). The Vampire Lestat Fan Club also hosts its coven ball on that weekend; venues change from year to year, and you must be a member to attend, although membership is open to everyone and is quite reasonable. For information,

I woke up just before dawn on Mardi Gras day, and I could hear the action on the street already. . . . I put on my Egyptian dancing girl outfit, and headed over to the Moonwalk, the boardwalk named for Moon Landrieu, opposite Jackson Square, to search for the apocryphal Krewe of Stella. I had heard about a group of college men—frat rats with a literary bent—who tried to emulate Marlon Brando's torn-T-shirt charisma as Stanley Kowalski in *A Streetcar Named Desire*. I wasn't sure the krewe actually existed, since no one I knew had ever managed to get up early enough to see them. . . .

When I arrived at the Moonwalk, a small crowd had already gathered. They were peering out at the river. A man wearing a feathered headdress and ill-fitting tuxedo suddenly yelled and pointed upriver at an object bobbing along on the current. "There they are!" It was a small rowboat painted green and purple, with a tattered banner attached to a stick, slowly heading toward the bank. The name *Stella* was painted crudely on the stern. There were two people aboard, along with a big yellow beer keg. As the boat washed ashore, a young man wearing a sheer white nightgown disembarked first, followed by a young man wearing an admiral's jacket, plumed hat, and plaid Bermuda shorts. . . .

The young man in the admiral's hat threw out his chest and squinched up his face, Brando style, yelling, in glorious agony, "Stel-la-a-a!"

A young man wearing a headband over his long hair teetered a bit on his feet as he watched. "He's living it," said the young man in an awed tone. "He's living the dream."

The crowd started moving across Decatur street to Jackson Square, two of them dragging the boat, and by the time they reach the Pontalba building, they were running, all of them yelling, "Stel-la-a-a," dozens of Brandos searching for solace, a horde of the lusty vulgarians Williams had envisioned as both the last hope and the destroyers of a refined and inbred culture. It was the end of Belle Reve and the debased dreams of Blanche DuBois and the last gasp of method acting.

—Carol Flake, *New Orleans: Behind the Masks of America's Most Exotic City*

write the Vampire Lestat Fan Club, P.O. Box 58277, New Orleans, LA 70158-58277. You can also call Rice's fan line at (504) 522-8634 for info or check out www.annerice.com.

THE NEW ORLEANS POPULAR FICTION CONFERENCE

Sponsored by the South Louisiana chapter of the Romance Writers of America, this one-day conference, usually held in November, is aimed at writers of genre fiction and draws a full array of romance, mystery, western, and science fiction writers, along with editors and agents. For conference information write NOPFC, P.O. Box 740113, New Orleans 70174-0113.

POETRY READINGS

The longest-running poetry series in the South keeps on trucking every Sunday at the Maple Leaf Bar, 8316 Oak Street. Readings begin at 3 P.M. Drop by, knock back a few, and bring your own poems in case there's an open-mike reading.

FOR MORE INFORMATION

Check the listings on the Sunday book page of the *Times-Picayune,* as well as its daily calendar listings, and Friday's Lagniappe entertainment section. The weekly newspaper *Gambit* also lists events; it hits the streets on Mondays.

The Maple Leaf Bar

From John Travis, ed., The Maple Leaf Rag: 15th Anniversary Anthology
(New Orleans: Portals Press, 1994), drawing by Jennie Kasten

They rode above the trees and rooftops of uptown to the right; to the left were the high-rise buildings of downtown, and ahead, not just the one she remembered but two bridges now stretching across the Mississippi. The taxi angled toward the St. Charles Avenue exit and approached her favorite landmark, the golden spire of St. John the Baptist, wet with sun. Thea's throat tightened and her vision blurred.

Her reaction startled her. She didn't like this city. There was too much squalor and chaos in it, decay and poverty were visible everywhere, neighborhoods jumbled, too much violence. She didn't like the people in New Orleans either. Their bonhomie was a smokescreen for their prurient curiosity, their politeness a wall of indifference to retreat behind. What they said was not what they meant; what they appeared to be was not what they were. Ultimately there were affected, narcissistic, dramatic. They used their nerves as their excuse. Michael called the people in New England tight-asses, but at least you knew where you stood with them, at least what you saw was what you got.

—Christine Wiltz, *Glass House*

Literary Resources

LIBRARIES

New Orleans Public Library
Web site: gnofn.org/~nopl (each branch also has a Web site)
The central branch of the library is downtown, and there are many others throughout the city, with changing exhibits and programming. The Main Library houses the African-American Resource Center (good for genealogical research). The Main Library's Louisiana Division (504-596-2610) is a reference resource devoted to the state and to the city of New Orleans. The division offers an extensive genealogy collection, the city archives, and the Carnival collection, as well as many other special collections. Library hours vary by location and by the current state of the city budget, so call ahead. Here are the branch locations and phone numbers:

Algiers Point
725 Pelican Ave.
(504) 596-2640

Algiers Regional
3014 Holiday Dr.
(504) 596-2642

Alvar
913 Alvar St.
(504) 596-2624

Broad Branch
4300 S. Broad St.
(504) 596-2675

Children's Resource Center
913 Napoleon Ave.
(504) 596-2628

East N.O. Regional
5641 Read Blvd.
(504) 596-2646

Gentilly
2098 Foy St.
(504) 596-2644

King
1617 Caffin Ave.
(504) 596-2695

Latter
5120 St. Charles Ave.
(504) 596-2625

Main Branch
219 Loyola Ave.
(504) 529-READ

Nix
401 S. Carrollton Ave.
(504) 596-2630

Nora Navra
1902 St. Bernard Ave.
(504) 596-2623

Smith Regional
6301 Canal Blvd.
(504) 596-2638

The Historic New Orleans Collection
533 Royal St.
New Orleans 70130
(504) 523-4662
Acting director: Priscilla Lawrence
Hours: Tuesday–Saturday 10 A.M.–4:45 P.M., Williams Gallery
10 A.M.–4:30 P.M., Williams Research Center (410 Chartres St.)
Tours of the history galleries and Williams residence
begin at 10 and 11 A.M. and 1 and 3 P.M. $4.

This lovely facility, founded by General and Mrs. L. Kemper Williams in 1966 and housed in elegant French Quarter buildings, is a rich and varied source for information on colonial Louisiana, the Louisiana Purchase, the Battle of New Orleans, the Civil War, Mississippi River life, cartography, transportation, plantations, urban development, Louisiana art and architecture, the French Quarter, Mardi Gras, and many other local and regional topics. The Williams Gallery features changing exhibits and frequent free public lectures, and has a wonderful gift and book shop with items you won't find anywhere else. The history galleries offer a brief introduction to three centuries of Louisiana history, and the Williams residence spotlights gracious twentieth-century living in the Quarter. The Williams Research Center, 410 Chartres St. (504-598-7171), shelters 14,000 volumes; 9,000 pamphlets; numerous documents and manuscripts; and approximately 300,000 photographs, prints, drawings, and paintings.

The facilities are pretty and comfortable, the staff pleasant and helpful. This is one of New Orleans's best collections, well worth a special trip.

Loyola University New Orleans Library
Loyola University
6363 St. Charles Ave.
New Orleans, LA 70118
(504) 865-3372
Librarian: Mary Lee Sweat
Special collections: Art Carpenter

The J. Edgar and Louise S. Monroe Library was dedicated in 1999, with holdings including the Frère Joseph-Aurelian Cornet archives. Cornet is one of the foremost experts on the art of the Congo, and his scholarship includes 150 field notebooks and 20,000 photographs. The library's rare books collection consists primarily of books about the Catholic Church, Louisiana, and New Orleans. The Walker Percy and His Circle Collection, begun in 1993 with a donation by Percy biographer Father Patrick Samway, contains books and material related to Walker Percy, Eudora Welty, Mary Lee Settle, Reynolds Price, and other southern writers. The library also has a collection of Lafcadio Hearn correspondence, H. L. Mencken letters, and the archives of the *New Orleans Review,* still being published by the Loyola English department. The new library building also houses the Lindy Boggs National Center for Community Literacy, with a focus on combating illiteracy and supporting literacy research and training teachers of reading.

Leonard S. Washington Memorial Library
Southern University at New Orleans
6400 Press Dr.
New Orleans, LA 70126
(504) 286-5224
Director: E. W. Young

Special holdings include an Afro-French Literature Collection and an African American Collection.

Howard-Tilton Memorial Library
Tulane University
7001 Freret St.
New Orleans, LA 70118-5862
(504) 865-5131
FAX: (504) 865-6773
Librarian: Phil Leinbach
E-mail: leinbach@mailhost.tcs.tulane.edu
Special Collections: Wilbur E. Meneray

The main library at Tulane University includes several important collections. The William Ransom Hogan Jazz Archive (Bruce Boyd

Raeburn is the expert here) is a great resource for music lovers and researchers. The Architecture Library, on the second floor of Richardson Memorial Hall, includes the Southeastern Architectural Archive, a treasure trove of New Orleans architecture with wonderful photographs. The Maxwell Music Library is an academic music library; the librarian is Dr. Robert Curtis, (504) 862-8645 or rcurtis@mailhost.tcs.tulane.edu. The Latin American Library, established in 1924, includes more than 320,000 volumes, as well as rare codices and other historical material. The Manuscripts Department is New Orleans's most comprehensive collection archive, with almost three linear miles of documents from the founding of New Orleans to the present. The collection has major resources on Carnival, the Civil War, Jewish studies, Louisiana politics, medical history, riverboats and waterways, and in many other areas. The library also has a strong Louisiana collection. Tulane's professional schools of medicine, business, and law also have extensive library holdings.

Two other Tulane research facilities:

Amistad Research Center
Tilton Hall, Tulane University
6823 St. Charles Ave.
New Orleans, LA 70118
Director: Donald E. DeVore
Membership info: (504) 862-3228
Fax (504) 865-5580
Web site: http://www.tulane.edu/~amistad
E-mail: arc@mailhost.tcs.tulane.edu

The 1839 rebellion of captive Africans aboard the Cuban slave ship *Amistad* has received wide recognition as a result of the Steven Spielberg film. Following the landmark Supreme Court case, which ended with a ruling declaring the freedom of the Africans, the defense committee gradually became the American Missionary Association, an important civil rights organization. Originally part of the Race Relations Department at Fisk University, this archive, founded by the American Missionary Association, moved to New

Orleans in 1969 and became an independent repository. This is one of the nation's largest African American history archives. Holdings date from the 1780s to the present, with more than 6,000 linear feet of primary documents, 250,000 photographs, an extensive oral history collection, 20,000 books, 30,000 pamphlets, an large periodical collection, and the Aaron Douglas Art Collection.

Nadine Vorhoff Library
Newcomb College Center for Research on Women
Caroline Richardson Hall
Tulane University
New Orleans, LA 70118-5683
(504) 865-5762

The Nadine Vorhoff Library, located in the Newcomb College Center for Research on Women, is the premier repository of feminist material in the city and has an oral history archive and a large cookbook collection. Each year, the center sponsors a Culinary Arts Symposium. The center also sponsors a variety of other programs, such as the Zale Writer-in-Residence program, which brings a noted writer to campus each fall for a full week of public lectures, classes and writing workshops. Susan Tucker is curator of Books and Records: susnnah@mailhost.tcs.tulane.edu.

Earl K. Long Library
The University of New Orleans
Lakefront
New Orleans, LA 70148
(504) 280-6556
Dean: Jill Fatzer
Archivist: Florence Jumonville

A trek out to UNO's Lakefront campus is rewarded with an interesting Louisiana archive, including the Marcus Christian papers and the work of the African American writers of the WPA, as well as special collections in Egyptology (Judge Pierre Crabites Collection), Louisiana history, William Faulkner (Frank A. Von der Haar Collection), and the archives and records of the Nuclear Regulatory Commission, the Orleans Parish School Board, and the Supreme Court of Louisiana.

The Xavier University of Louisiana Library
7325 Palmetto St.
New Orleans, LA 70125
(504) 483-7304
FAX: (504) 485-7917
University Librarian: Robert Skinner
E-mail: rskinner@xula.edu

The Xavier University of Louisiana Library's special collections are in the areas of black studies (the Negro History and Culture Collection), southern and black Catholicism, and southern writers.

Will W. Alexander Library
Dillard University
2601 Gentilly Blvd.
New Orleans, LA 70122-3097
(504) 286-4784
Director: Theodosia T. Shields

This library's special collections include resources on literature and architecture and the McPherson Memorial Freedom Collection.

AGENCIES

Arts Council of New Orleans
225 Baronne St.
Suite 1712
New Orleans, LA 70112
(504) 523-1465
E-mail: acno@acadiacom.net
Executive director: Shirley Trusty Corey

The Arts Council of New Orleans presents programs aimed at working artists, arts organizations, and arts administrators throughout the city. Write for membership and program information. Services include guidance in grant applications and the funding process, volunteer lawyers in the arts, and specific workshops such as stress management techniques. Most of the council's programs, however, are aimed at visual artists—particularly those involved in the new Louisiana Artists Guild, which will provide a mixed-use facility for working artists and a showcase for their work.

The Louisiana Division of the Arts
P.O. Box 44247
Baton Rouge, LA 70804-4247
(225) 342-8180
FAX (225) 342-8173
E-mail: arts@crt.state.la.us
Web site: http://www.crt.state.la.us
Executive director: James Borders

The Louisiana Division of the Arts is the state's official arts agency. It administers state and federal funds appropriated for arts grants, awarding approximately $4 million annually to state artists and nonprofit organizations. The agency offers fellowships and mini-grants to creative writers. Write for guidelines and deadlines. Staff is available to assist with the technicalities of applying; James Borders administers the programs in literature.

The Louisiana Endowment for the Humanities
225 Baronne St.
Suite 1414
New Orleans, LA 70112-1783
(504) 523-4352
or statewide (800) 909-7990
FAX (504) 529-2358
e-mail: leh@leh.org.
Executive director: Michael Sartisky

The Louisiana Endowment for the Humanities, the state affiliate of the National Endowment for the Humanities, offers broad-based support for humanities activities. In addition to its other programs, the LEH sponsors two special funding programs for writers.

One program entails grants for publication and/or photodocumentation. There are four grants of up to $2,500 in support of Louisiana writers working with Louisiana-related topics in literature, history, language, music, cultural anthropology, folklife, or other humanities areas. In addition the LEH offers up to three grants of $2,500 for the photodocumentation of Louisiana culture. All projects culminate in the creation of a manuscript, which must be submitted to close the grant. Projects must be of interest to a general audience; scholarly monographs are not eligible. Criteria include quality, originality, accessibility to or appropriateness for the general public, likelihood or proximity of publication, and plans for distribution. Eligible costs include stipends, clerical expenses, travel, books, photocopying, photography, and other direct project costs. Applications are screened by a panel of scholars and experts. The LEH board makes the final awards. Call for applications and deadlines.

The other program is the Louisiana Publishing Initiative, intended to increase the quality and quantity of books published on general-interest Louisiana humanities topics. The LEH offers grants of up to $10,000. An author or a publisher may apply, but all applicants are required to have a sponsoring nonprofit organization. The applicant must clearly demonstrate the humanities content as well as the topic's relationship to Louisiana in the proposal. Photography must be documentary.

There are two important points to bear in mind. First, the LEH does not fund the writing of fiction. Second, call before making an application. Staff members can advise you about the chances of funding for your project and guide you in grant preparation. They will review drafts received four to six weeks before deadlines.

The LEH also publishes the magazine *Cultural Vistas*.

LITERARY AGENTS

The Ahearn Agency
2021 Pine St.
New Orleans, LA 70118
(504) 861-8395

Agent Pamela Ahearn is known for representing local romance writers but is also the agent for the extremely successful mystery novelist Laura Joh Rowland and has represented nonfiction writers. Must query first.

The Harris Literary Agency
2233 St. Charles Ave., Suite 710
New Orleans, LA 70130
(504) 561-0549

Attorney Cindy Harris-Williams, who is the author of several romance novels, is interested in submissions of book-length fiction.

PUBLISHERS

Louisiana State University Press
P.O. Box 25053
Baton Rouge, LA 70894-5053
(225) 388-6666
Director: L. E. Phillabaum
Editor in chief: Maureen Hewitt

Founded in 1935, Louisiana State University Press publishes primarily academic and scholarly books of regional interest, along with some general-interest titles. Areas of special interest are southern and United States history, African American history, and Civil War history, as well as art, architecture, photography, southern literature, European literature, general literary criticism, music, natural history, and poetry. Query letters and SASEs should be addressed to Maureen Hewitt, editor in chief.

Pelican Publishing
P.O. Box 3110
Gretna, LA 70053
(504) 368-1175
Publisher: Dr. Milburn Calhoun

Founded in 1926, Pelican publishes primarily nonfiction of general trade interest, with a specialty in travel books and titles of regional interest. Query letters and SASEs should be sent to Milburn Calhoun, publisher.

Portals Press of New Orleans
4411 Fontainebleau
New Orleans, LA 70125
Publisher: John Travis
Published *The Maple Leaf Rag: 15th Anniversary Anthology.* Query.

Runagate Press
P.O. Box 52723
New Orleans, LA 70152-2723
Editor: Kysha Brown
This publisher has a dual focus: books on New Orleans culture and on African heritage cultures worldwide. Query first.

B. E. Trice Publishing
2727 Prytania
New Orleans, LA 70130
Publisher: Britton Trice
Publishes beautiful limited editions of works by well-known authors, Anne Rice and James Lee Burke among them.

Xavier Review Press
Xavier University
7325 Palmetto St.
Box 110C
New Orleans, LA 70125-1098
Editors: Thomas Bonner Jr. and Robert Skinner
This press occasionally publishes full-length books by authors whose work has appeared in the *Xavier Review,* as well as anthologies of poetry (*Immortelles*) and fiction (*Above Ground*) by southern writers. Query first.

WRITING GROUPS

The Nommo Literary Society
P.O. Box 52723
New Orleans, LA 70152-2723
Phone: (504) 581-2963

Nommo takes its name from the Swahili word for "song." Begun in 1985, the group grew out of writing workshops held at Southern University in New Orleans and gradually evolved into a multifaceted literary organization devoted to educating the next generation of African American writers in New Orleans. Kalamu ya Salaam is the founder. A writers' workshop meets every Tuesday at 6 P.M. at the group's headquarters at 1110 Tremé St. Members pay annual dues to belong. Sessions are a rigorous combination of study, networking, reading, and critique. Nommo also sponsors occasional book discussion groups and regular public readings at 7 P.M. the second Friday of every month at Community Book Center, 219 N. Broad St. Members of the group are also in charge of its publishing arm, Runagate Press, and the Tremé School of Writing, currently in the planning stages.

The Society of Children's Book Writers and Illustrators

Aimed at aspiring writers of books for children, this group meets monthly with programming and critique groups. It also sponsors writing workshops. Contact: Carrel Muller at (504) 282-4660.

SOLA: The South Louisiana Chapter
of the Romance Writers of America
P.O. Box 6752
Metairie, LA 70009-6752

This is one of the largest, most welcoming writers' groups in the city. Despite its name, the organization attracts writers of all kinds of books to its monthly meetings, which feature a broad array of useful programming. SOLA sponsors the New Orleans Popular Fiction Conference in the fall and publishes a monthly newsletter. Prospective members are invited to attend two consecutive meetings before joining. To become a member of SOLA, you must be a member of the Romance Writers of America. Annual SOLA dues are $22; annual RWA dues are $60, with a first-year processing fee of $10.

The New Orleans Poetry Forum

Founded in 1971, this writers' group meets weekly at 8 P.M. at the Broad branch of the New Orleans Public Library, 4300 S. Broad. Bring fifteen copies of a poem to critique. Annual dues are $15. The forum has also sponsored public readings (including an appearance by former member and 1994 Pulitzer Prize winner Yusef Komunyakaa, author of *Neon Vernacular*), guest lectures in local schools, and poetry workshops in prisons. For many years the group sponsored the publication of the *New Laurel Review,* and since 1995 it has published an electronic magazine, *Desire Street.* For more information, e-mail Andrea Gereighty at Ager80@worldnet.att.net.

LITERARY SOCIETY

The Pirate's Alley Faulkner Society
632 Pirate's Alley
New Orleans, LA 70116-3254
(504) 586-1612
Web site: http://members.aol.com/faulkhouse

The Pirate's Alley Faulkner Society sponsors the annual celebration Words and Music: A Literary Feast in New Orleans, a festival for writers and literary tourists. This event includes the society's annual meeting and celebration, "Happy Birthday, Mr. Faulkner," each September. Membership is $25 for students, $50 for individuals, $100 for "special friends," $150 for "patrons," $500 for "sponsors," and $1,000 for "sustaining members." Membership includes an annual subscription to the *Double Dealer Redux,* the society's journal.

The society also sponsors the William Faulkner Creative Writing Competition. There are six divisions—novels, novellas, short stories, personal essays, poetry, and high school short stories. Winners receive their awards (generous cash prizes and commemorative medals) at the Faulkner birthday celebration. Write the society for guidelines and entry forms or download them from the Web site.

PUBLICATIONS

Most of the following publications are available
at area bookstores and newsstands:

Cultural Vistas. This is the publication of the Louisiana Endowment for the Humanities and showcases the work of the endowment and its scholars. It features book excerpts, interviews with writers, original fiction and poetry, and photography.

Exquisite Corpse. Edited by poet and NPR commentator Andrei Codrescu, this journal formerly published at Louisiana State University is now on-line at www.exquisitecorpse.org.

Louisiana Literature. Published by the English Department at Southeastern Louisiana University, this is an exceptionally fine literary journal.

New Laurel Review. Founded by Paul and Alice Claudel, this is a journal of original fiction and poetry, edited by poet and short-story writer Lee Meitzen Grue. Published intermittently.

New Orleans Review. Published by the English Department at Loyola University, this longtime favorite offers a broad selection of local writing, including fiction, poetry, photography, reviews, and interviews.

Southern Review. Published at Louisiana State University in Baton Rouge, this is one of the oldest and most distinguished literary journals in the country.

Xavier Review. Published by Xavier University and edited by Thomas Bonner Jr. and Robert Skinner, this review features a variety of original work and scholarship, with an emphasis on African American studies.

When I tasted the jambalaya I then could tell why it had achieved the status, through lore, of a holy food. . . . Hoodoo Food. Syncretic: Spanish, African, native American, French—adaptable to all cultures. There was warm fellowship in this restaurant. The waiters and waitresses talked in a slow hum of good will. . . . A hum that could put you to sleep. This was the sweet South of ambrosia, where people say yes mah'm and no mah'm, where there's always the best silver layed [sic] out, and places set in case somebody stops by hungry. . . .

A land where the male leads are played by Clark Gable and Don Ameche, tipping their top hats, and escorting ladies to the ice cream parlor. And New Orleans is the thick cream of that sweet South. The South's vanilla. The city of po boy sandwiches, Frankie and Johnny, Louis Armstrong, the great Zulu, where the mayor's first name is Moon and every day a Frank Yerby novel. If you're a tourist they'll show you where Tennessee Williams lives and gossip about Clay Shaw. (Had whips in his closet!)

—Ishmael Reed, "Shrovetide in Old New Orleans"

Lagniappe: Writers' Favorites

Doug Brinkley's History Highlights

1. Jackson Square and its surround. It's such a key place in the city, with the Monument, the River, the Pontalba Buildings.
2. Preservation Hall
3. The French Market
4. Gallier Hall
5. Chalmette Battlefield National Cemetery
6. St. Louis Cemetery No. 1, with all the voodoo history, part of our Caribbean heritage
7. Congo Square, Storyville, Louis Armstrong Park
8. St. Charles Streetcar—the streetcar itself is a national historic site.
9. Pirate's Alley and Faulkner House, for its literary associations
10. Beauregard-Keyes House, because it combines literary and Civil War history

Susan Larson's Literary Fun for Little Ones

If you're a booklover traveling to New Orleans with children, don't miss Storyland in City Park. You can climb on Captain Hook's ship, venture into the mouth of the whale with Pinocchio, and clamber into or admire any number of sites from nursery rhymes and tales. The web of Miss Muffet's spider is there for the climbing, Mother Goose is flying overhead, and you can even imagine living in that crooked little house. All for an admission of $2, which often includes story times. Don't forget to take a camera—the family photo opportunities are wonderful. City Park offers other attractions for children and adults: the New Orleans Museum of Art and the New Orleans Botanical Gardens are there, as well as a small amusement park with a truly magnificent carousel.

RICK BARTON'S TEN FAVORITE NEW ORLEANS FILMS

Barton is a novelist and the film critic for *Gambit* (the protagonist in his novel *With Extreme Prejudice* is a movie critic as well).

Jezebel. William Wyler (1938)
Panic in the Streets. Elia Kazan (1950)
A Streetcar Named Desire. Elia Kazan (1951)
Easy Rider. Dennis Hopper (1969)
Hard Times. Walter Hill (1975)
Pretty Baby. Louis Malle (1977)
Tightrope. Richard Tuggle (1984)
Down by Law. Jim Jarmusch (1986)
Wild at Heart. David Lynch (1990)
Dead Man Walking. Tim Robbins (1995)

"And despite its ludicrous accents and pathetic sense of local geography, purely for its story and performances, I liked Jim McBride's *The Big Easy* (1986). I also very much liked John Sayles's *Passion Fish* (1993), but it's not really about New Orleans."

CHRISTINE WILTZ'S FIVE FAVORITE CRIME SCENES

Wiltz, a crime novelist and biographer (*The Last Madam*), shares the best places to catch a glimpse of criminal activity in New Orleans:

1. *Partying with politicos*—lots of crawfish, booze, women, porno flicks, and big-money deals. The crawfish and booze are legal; so are some of the women. Porno flicks are questionable—the city ordinance on obscenity is wide open to interpretation. But the deals can come back to haunt you.

2. *Sword fighting by firelight.* Dueling is no longer legal in New Orleans, but blood still stains the earth under the Dueling Oaks in City Park.

3. *Chicken drop contests in West Bank barrooms.* As the chicken prances around the big board on the floor, bet your favorite number and hope the chicken drops on it. But beware of animal rights activists.

4. *High stakes poker games in French Quarter back rooms*—traveler beware.

5. *Cockfights.* Cockfighting is legal in Louisiana, but making book on the fights is not. Not many gamblers try that, though, because it's legal to bet head-to-head. The highest incidence of crime surrounding cockfighting is the theft of champion roosters.

JASON BERRY'S MUST-HAVE MUSIC

Berry, author of *Up from the Cradle of Jazz* and many other works, chooses the indispensable New Orleans CDs:

Louis Armstrong and His Hot 5 and Hot 7, 1926–1927. Classics 585
Louis Armstrong Gospel, 1931–1941. F & A 001
Sidney Bechet, 1924–43. RPCD 632
The Jelly Roll Morton Centennial. RCA Bluebird 2361-2-RB
Eureka Brass Band: New Orleans Funeral and Street Parade. AMCD 70
Johnny Adams: Good Morning Heartache. Rounder 2125
Zion Harmonizers: Best of New Orleans Gospel, Vol. 2. MGR 108
Louis Prima, Collector Series. CDP 7940722
The Wild Tchoupitoulas. Mango 162-539 908-2
Paul Barbarin and His New Orleans Band: Streets of the City. 504 CD 9
Henry "Red" Allen and His Orchestra, 1929–1933. Classics 540
Donald Harrison Jr.: Indian Blue, featuring The Guardians of the Flame Mardi Gras Indians and Dr. John. CCD 79514

Mardi Gras in New Orleans. MG 1001
Majesty of the Blues: Wynton Marsalis Sextet. Columbia 38641
Antoine "Fats" Domino: 25 Classic Performances. EMI 52326
Loved Ones: Ellis and Branford Marsalis. CK 67369
Professor Longhair: Houseparty New Orleans Style. Rounder 2057
Dr. John: Gumbo. Atlantic CD 7006
The Neville Brothers: Yellow Moon. A & M 5240

VIETNAM ON THE BAYOU

Robert Olen Butler received critical acclaim and a Pulitzer Prize for his short-story collection *A Good Scent from a Strange Mountain,* which is about Vietnamese immigrants and is set partly in a Vietnamese enclave called Versailles in eastern New Orleans. For a glimpse of this other world, you can go to the Saturday open-air market, but be warned that it's all over by 9 A.M., so this is for early birds only. To get there, take I-10 east and exit on Chef Menteur, heading east. Take a left on Alcée Fortier Blvd. (you'll notice the many Vietnamese stores and restaurants). In the courtyard of the apartment complex two blocks back on the left, there's an open-air market with local produce, sandwiches, plants, and crafts. Watch for the truck parked on Alcée Fortier with live chickens and ducks for sale. If you venture down Dwyer Boulevard, you'll see traditional Vietnamese gardens that will make you think you're in another country.

TONY DUNBAR'S GOURMET GUIDE

New Orleans mystery novelist Tony Dunbar's detective Tubby Dubonnet savors New Orleans food in every mouth-watering book. Here are some of Dunbar's favorite places to eat:

Ditcharo's Pasta and Sandwiches
116 Tulane Ave.

Crescent City Steak House
1001 N. Broad

Bar at Ye Olde College Inn (not the restaurant, the bar)
3016 S. Carrollton

Guy's Poorboy's
5257 Magazine St.

Julie Smith's Lo-Cal Locales

Smith's homicide detective Skip Langdon worries about her weight, so she recommends:

Samurai Sushi
609 Decatur St.
Always a good bet, especially since tourists steer clear of it. Who comes to New Orleans to eat Japanese?

Remoulade
309 Bourbon St.
An offshoot of Arnaud's. Skip goes there for the raw oysters, boiled shrimp, and crawfish. They have nice salads too.

The Praline Connection
542 Frenchmen St.
For the greens and rice.

Old Dog–New Trick Café
307 Exchange Alley
Skip's a vegetarian, so her unvarying choice is the Tofu-rama.

Café Degas
3127 Esplanade Ave.
For the vegetable melange.

Poppy Z. Brite's Rules for Eating in New Orleans

1. Anything you eat in a restaurant is not fattening, because you will work it off by getting up from the table and leaving the restaurant.

2. A calorie is a unit of heat; therefore, frozen desserts have no calories.

3. Seafood is health food, even if it's surrounded by three times its weight in batter and grease.

4. The dill pickle slice that comes with your fried seafood platter counts as a vegetable.

5. Gumbo is a major food group.

6. No one will be offended if you order the Wop salad—but don't buy Commie crawfish!

THE DEAD ZONE

Best cemetery spots, by Sandra Russell Clark and Patricia Brady, authors of *Elysium—A Gathering of Souls: New Orleans Cemeteries:*

Wandering though the haphazard aisles of St. Louis Cemetery 1, you come across a fresh delight every time you turn a corner— from the tomb of voodoo priestess Marie Laveau to Governor Claiborne's monuments to his (successive) Protestant and Catholic wives, almost within touching distance of each other.

Two of our favorite tombs are in this old colonial cemetery. The Bergamini tomb is a classic double-vaulted house of the dead. Kneeling atop it is the mourning figure of a young girl, her face nearly worn away by tears, the image of Lafcadio Hearn's "dead face that asked for a kiss."

In the same cemetery is the beautiful white marble Italian Society Tomb, its graceful baroque curves dancing in the midst of somber rectangular monuments. Immigrants who died far from home are interred in its twenty-four vaults.

St. Louis 2, the city's echo of Paris's Père Lachaise, is home to the Barelli tomb, whose namesake isn't buried there—or anywhere. A marble bas-relief memorializes young Joseph Barelli, blown sky-high by an exploding steamboat. His watch lying on the levee was the only trace left behind.

Metairie Cemetery is the ultimate in Victorian grandeur with its garden setting, formerly a race track, and its truly monumental tombs. But even among these grandiose mortuary fantasies, Lucien Brunswig's Egyptian pyramid, guarded by a statuesque female figure and a watchful sphinx, stands out.

Holt Cemetery, where many jazz greats lie in unmarked graves, drowses like a weedy country cemetery under live oak trees. Pearl S. Landry's grave is simple and touching with its hand-carved wooden tombstone decorated with flowers and a cross.

PATTY FRIEDMANN'S SMELL-O-RAMA

Novelist Friedmann recalls "smells from my New Orleans childhood that make Combray seem positively antiseptic":

1. The molasses factory at the foot of Broadway (now Uptown Square)

2. The drugstore in the basement at the Edgewater Beach Hotel (between Gulfport and Biloxi; a shopping center now stands on the site)

3. The Lusher School cafeteria on Mondays

4. The Sunbeam Bakery as we passed it on the Expressway

5. The inside of the streetcar in the summer

ROBERT OLEN BUTLER AND ELIZABETH DEWBERRY RECOMMEND ROMANCE

Robert Olen Butler and his wife, novelist Elizabeth Dewberry *(Many Things Have Happened since He Died; Break the Heart of Me)*, often come to New Orleans for a romantic weekend.

1. After sleeping late and drinking your coffee together on your hotel balcony—our favorite is the Bienville House, with a balcony overlooking Decatur—take a stroll along the Moonwalk by the

Mississippi River. Find a nice bench, hold hands, listen to the street musicians, and do some people watching. We like to pick out couples and make up their stories together—what attracts them to each other, what brought them to New Orleans, what kind of life they'll go back to when they leave. After you've watched a few tugboats and ships pass by in front of you, hop on the Mississippi River ferry and take a ride yourself. It goes to Algiers and back, but don't bother getting off in Algiers.

2. By now, you're getting hungry. Wander through the Quarter to the Napoleon House for a leisurely early lunch. Get a table in one of the huge open windows, where you're half in the restaurant, half on the sidewalk. It's a beautiful, shabby old building that serves wonderful jambalaya and muffalettas. Top your meal off with some of their exquisite Italian ice.

3. Spend the next couple of hours antiquing and art-gallery-hopping on Royal and Chartres Streets. If you have the money, you can get some of the most romantic antique jewelry in the world here, and if you don't, it's still romantic to window shop.

4. When you're ready to rest your feet, buy ice cream cones at the Häagen-Dazs just behind St. Louis Cathedral and bring them to Jackson Square to watch people and listen to street musicians while you eat. If you want to have your fortune told, our favorite soothsayer is Hubba Bubba. He's huge and he wears a big turban, so if he's there, you can't miss him. Don't forget to peek in St. Louis Cathedral before you leave.

5. Head down Pirate's Alley to Faulkner House Books, where Faulkner lived and wrote his second novel. It's a booklover's bookstore, with lots of wonderful novels and some extraordinary first editions. Buy something set in New Orleans to read to each other when you get home.

6. It's late afternoon by now, and if you're ready for a drink, go to the Sazerac Bar in the Fairmont Hotel, just on the other side of

Canal, and order Sazeracs. This is the classic New Orleans bar, with live piano music, big, plush sofas, and a wonderful mural by Paul Ninas. Ask the pianist to play your song—it's corny, but it's still romantic.

7. Walk back through the Quarter on Bourbon Street, which is just waking up this time of day. When you find yourself directly behind St. Louis Cathedral, stop in the intersection and look down the street at the shadow on the wall, a huge silhouette of Jesus with his arms outstretched. The juxtaposition of it and the Bourbon Street scene is quintessential New Orleans, and very moving. Then stop in Marie Laveau's House of Voodoo for a love potion, or at least a voodoo doll refrigerator magnet.

8. Keep wandering in the Quarter until you get to the G & E Grill on Decatur. Ask for a seat in the courtyard, not too near the open-air rotisserie (unless it's a cool evening). The candlelit atmosphere is elegant without being pretentious, and the meals are delicious and imaginative without being strange, so you get to try some new things, but still eat something that feels like comfort food. We love a lot of New Orleans restaurants, but this is probably our favorite.

9. Walk the rest of the way down Decatur, cross Esplanade, and turn left on Frenchmen Street. Between Royal and Chartres, you'll find the Snug Harbor Jazz Bistro, an intimate little club that always has wonderful jazz, often with names the uninitiated will recognize. They offer shows at nine and eleven, but the nine o'clock show tends to draw a quieter, more romance-minded crowd, where the later show often has more partyers. You can buy your tickets in advance, but seating is always first-come, first-served, so get there a little early. We always try for the second table from the front on the left-hand wall, when you're facing the stage. It's the best place for watching the musicians and the audience at once.

10. As you stroll back to the Bienville House, stop for beignets and coffee at the Café du Monde, but leave room for one last glass of champagne, to be sipped on your balcony in the hotel while you toast your day.

I see in Mardi Gras much what I hear in a really good jazz band: a model for the just society, the joyous community, the heavenly city. I see a recurring ritual devoted to spontaneity, a festival in which collective display is impossible without individual creativity, a form in which innovation is grounded in tradition. In short, a model for community where individual expression is the basis for creativity. and, despite considerable evidence to the contrary, I trust I will find in my home town the creativity and good humor that will allow the best to endure, even if it must endure side by side with old troubles that should be long gone and human failings that will last till Gabriel's horn. Few people in New Orleans look for the millennium, but when the millennium comes, it will look a lot like New Orleans.

—Reid Mitchell, *All on a Mardi Gras Day*

Jackson Square was desolate. I didn't know if that was the way it always was at that time of night, because I'd never been there before at that hour. It was so quiet that I thought if we stopped sliding our shoes over the bricks we might be able to hear the clock ticking at St. Louis Cathedral. Straight ahead lay Cafe du Monde. I was tired from the trek from one end of the Quarter to the other and, I guess, from the weight of the evening, so I was anticipating the rush of sugar from the beignets and the caffeine from the coffee. Gray seemed even more eager than I was. His pace was quickening with each step. We were both smiling, somewhat mischievously I couldn't help feeling, like two youngsters who, after having been sent to bed by their parents, had climbed out of the upstairs window and down the drainpipe, preferring, to sleep, a more literal nocturnal adventure. And walking to the river though the middle of the French Quarter, as we were doing now, always gave me the palpable sensation of advancing toward the very beginning of the city, tracing the steps of progress. Maybe it was this easy access to the distant past—available upon the merest of whims and at the slight expense of the most casual of strolls—that gave the city its perpetual aura of antiquity. Hand in hand, Gray and I jogged across Decatur Street and took a couple of steps into the cafe.

High above us, the ceiling fans were whirling, yes, *whirling*, not merely on, not simply turning, and they drew us into the cafe like misinformed men lured to Casablanca by rumors of the waters.

—Louis Edwards, *N*

Beyond New Orleans

NEW ORLEANS ISN'T the only place where writers live and work in Louisiana, though some would certainly argue that it's the best place to be. But towns and cities small and large throughout the state have their share of writers, past and present. The state's literature reflects its diverse culture, its unfolding history.

Baton Rouge, the state capital, is home to many writers and historians. A drive to the campus of Louisiana State University is an enjoyable day trip. The university also boasts a well-regarded creative writing program and the prestigious journal *Southern Review,* and any lover of books can spend a happy afternoon at Hill Memorial Library.

Ernest Gaines, who reached a worldwide audience through the novel and subsequent film of *The Autobiography of Miss Jane Pittman,* was born and raised on False River near New Roads (how could you not become a writer with those names marking the homeplace?). Today he divides his time among Miami, San Francisco, and Lafayette, where he teaches a creative writing seminar each fall at the University of Southwestern Louisiana.

Bogalusa, in Washington Parish, is the hometown of Yusef Komunyakaa, who received the 1994 Pulitzer Prize for his poetry collection *Neon Vernacular.*

Another African American poet born in Louisiana was Arna Bontemps (1902–1973). A major figure of the Harlem Renaissance who wrote about the lives and struggles of black Americans, Bontemps is also noted for the anthologies *The Poetry of the Negro* (1949) and *The Book of Negro Folklore* (1948), both edited with Langston Hughes. Today his home in Alexandria is a museum.

Cajun storytellers are legendary, and with good reason, spinning the simplest life event into the most amusing, moving and complicated tale. Tim Gautreaux, who is writer-in-residence at Southeastern Louisiana University in Hammond, dryly charms and moves readers with his stories of modern-day Cajuns. The settings of his novel *The Next Step in the Dance* and most of the pieces in his short-story collections *Same Place, Same Things* and *Welding with Children* might be almost any small town in south. Gautreaux lives in the Hammond woods in an Acadian cottage, his love for machinery evident in the tractors, train lanterns, and whistles he collects.

Another great chronicler of Cajun culture is novelist Albert Belisle Davis, who lives in Thibodaux and is novelist-in-residence at Nicholls State University there. Davis's first two novels, *Leechtime* and *Marquis at Bay,* are the first and second volumes in his projected Mondebon trilogy. Davis's fictional vision of the communities around Mondebon Bayou also resulted in a volume of poetry, *What They Wrote on the Bathhouse Walls.*

Perhaps the best known of all Cajun characters in fiction is James Lee Burke's detective Dave Robicheaux. Both character and creator make their home in New Iberia. Burke's moral dramas have deep roots in the political and racial history of the region. And his love of the land itself is reflected in memorable descriptive passages that read like poetry.

Lake Charles is the hometown of Pulitzer Prize winner Robert Olen Butler, who received the award for his 1993 collection of short stories *A Good Scent from a Strange Mountain.* Butler, who teaches at McNeese State University, has often said how much the south Louisiana landscape reminds him of Vietnam.

Farther north, in Shreveport, which many south Louisianians like to joke is really just a suburb of Dallas, lives and works the talented artist/author William Joyce. Joyce has received wide recognition for such innovative books for children as *A Day with Wilbur Robinson, Bently and Egg, Santa Calls, Nicholas Cricket,* and *Buddy,* as well as for his work on such films as *Buddy* and *Toy Story.*

Here are some literary landmarks beyond New Orleans that are well worth a visit:

ALEXANDRIA

Arna Bontemps African-American Museum
and Cultural Arts Center
1327 Third St.
Alexandria, LA 71301
(318) 473-4692

Open Tuesday–Friday, 10 A.M.–4 P.M., Saturday 10 A.M.–2 P.M. This 1890 frame house was the boyhood home of the poet. The Louisiana Black Hall of Fame is also located here. Bontemps described his attachment to the place in an essay titled "Why I Returned." Bontemps was the author of three novels, edited several anthologies, and wrote works for younger readers.

Bentley Hotel
200 De Soto
Alexandria, LA 71301
(318) 448-9600 or (800) 356-6835

This gorgeous hotel, built in 1908, is worth a trip just to see the restored lobby with its stained-glass dome. The neoclassical building, its Beaux Arts interior beautifully restored, is the hotel described in *Ritz of the Bayou,* Nancy Lemann's book about the 1986 corruption trial of Governor Edwin Edwards. In the days of Huey Long, the Bentley was a favorite crossroads for Louisiana politicians' meeting and scheming.

ANGOLA

Louisiana State Penitentiary
Angola, LA 70712
(225) 655-4411

The famous maximum security prison is the setting for Sister Helen Prejean's memoir *Dead Man Walking.* It also figures importantly in several of James Lee Burke's Dave Robicheaux novels. The prison is not open for tours, but every Sunday in October there's a prison rodeo featuring craft sales by inmate artisans. The Angola rodeo was the subject of journalist Dan Bergner's *God of the Rodeo*

(Knopf, 1998). Inmate Wilbert Rideau, who founded the prison newspaper the *Angolite,* has gained a reputation as a writer on the criminal justice system.

BATON ROUGE

Hill Memorial Library
LSU Campus
Baton Rouge, LA 70803
(225) 388-6551
Monday–Friday, 9 A.M.–5 P.M., Saturday by appointment
A wonderful special collection of Louisiana material. Don't miss Knute Heldner's WPA mural.

Louisiana State Archives Building
3851 Essen
Baton Rouge, LA 70804
(225) 922-1206
Monday–Friday, 8 A.M.–4:30 P.M., Saturday 9 A.M.–5 P.M.,
Sunday 1–5 P.M. Free.
Changing exhibits document state history, drawing on this archival collection of newspapers, letters, and other primary materials.

Louisiana State Capitol Building
State Capitol Dr.
Baton Rouge, LA 70804
(225) 342-7317
Daily 8 A.M.–4:30 P.M. Free.
This gorgeous art deco building, constructed during the Huey Long administration, is the tallest state capitol building in the United States. Long was assassinated here in 1935, and he is buried beneath a statue on the grounds. Visit the gift shop and the observation deck on the twenty-seventh floor.

Old State Capitol
100 North Boulevard
Baton Rouge, LA 70801

(225) 342-0500
or 800-488-2968
Tuesday–Saturday, 10 A.M.–4 P.M., Sunday, noon-4. Admission
Now the Center for Political and Governmental History, this is
repository for historic documents and memorabilia. The 1849 capitol is a gorgeous and romantic building. See *Louisiana's Capitols:
The Beauty and the Glory,* by photographer Phillip Gould and Tulane University historian Lawrence N. Powell, for great reading
about and pictures of the two buildings.

CLOUTIERVILLE

Kate Chopin House and Bayou Folk Museum
243 La. Hwy. 495
Cloutierville, LA 71416
(318) 379-2233 or 357-7907
Monday–Saturday 10 A.M.–5 P.M., Sunday, 1–5 P.M. Admission.
Kate Chopin's husband's family was in business in Cloutierville,
and she lived in this village in Natchitoches Parish between 1879
and 1884 before moving to St. Louis and starting her writing career. She drew on her experiences here for *Bayou Folk* and *Nights
in Acadie.*

The Kate Chopin home was established in 1965 by Mildred
McCoy as the Bayou Folk Museum; McCoy, a lifelong resident of
the town, designed the museum as a tribute to the bayou folk and
the woman who brought them to literary light. It is a National Historical Landmark as well as a Louisiana Landmark. Exhibits on
Chopin's life and work, as well as Cane River history, are a feature.

MONROE

Bible Museum
2006 Riverside
Monroe, LA 71201
(318) 387-5281
or (800) 362-0983
Tuesday–Friday 10 A.M.–4 P.M., Saturday and Sunday, 2–5 P.M. Free

Established in 1971, this museum includes many priceless early Bibles from the collection of Emy-Lou Biedenharn, who returned home to Monroe after her career as an opera singer in Europe was cut short by the Second World War. Her husband, Joseph Biedenharn, was the first person to bottle Coca-Cola. She died in 1984. Among the items in the collection are an 1848 facsimile of the New Testament translated into English by John Wycliffe, a 1730 Martin Luther Bible, a 1611 King James Bible, an 1850 Victorian psalter, and a Bible illustrated by Salvador Dali, as well as a leaf from a Gutenberg Bible. Biedenharn's home and its grounds, the ELsong Gardens, are also open to the public.

MELROSE

Melrose Plantation
Exit 119 off I-49
Melrose, LA 71452
(318) 379-0055
Open daily noon–4 P.M. Admission.

Melrose Plantation, roughly fifteen miles south of Natchitoches, Louisiana, was built by a freed slave named Marie Thérèse, known as "Coincoin," who received land and freedom from Thomas Pierre Metoyer, a French merchant who was the father of her ten children. After arts patron Cammie Henry took possession in the early twentieth century, she made the house a welcome destination for writers and artists. Lyle Saxon often retreated to a cottage at Melrose to write. Other famous guests included Erskine Caldwell, William Faulkner, Rachel Field, John Steinbeck, and Alexander Woollcott. Art lovers know Melrose as the home of Clementine Hunter, the "black Grandma Moses," acclaimed for her primitive paintings, some of which are displayed at the African House on the plantation. (Hunter was a cook for Mrs. Henry and her guests.)

NATCHITOCHES

The Book Merchant
512 Front Street

Natchitoches, LA 71457
(318) 357-8900
Owner: J. Michael Kenny

New Iberia

Home to Cajun detective Dave Robicheaux, as well as his creator, James Lee Burke, New Iberia abounds with sights from Burke's novels, including Bayou Teche. As Burke says, "You know, they say that if you drink from the Bayou Teche, you'll never leave," so think carefully before you do.

If Burke's novels put your taste buds on alert, try the Bon Creole Lunch Counter at 1409 E. St. Peter (318) 367-6181, Lagniappe Too at 204 E. Main (318) 365-9491, or Victor's Cafeteria at 109 W. Main (318) 369-9924 (you'll know Victor's by the "Dave Eats Here" sign). Stroll the town to soak up the atmosphere. You can stop in at Books along the Teche for a "Robicheaux's Dock and Bait Shop" t-shirt or fishing cap, although there is no actual address to go along with it. You'll have to check out the fishing camps and bayous on your own. For more information, write or call Iberia Parish Tourist Information at (318) 365-1540.

Books along the Teche
110 East Main
New Iberia, LA 70560
(318) 367-7621
FAX (318) 367-7621
Owners: Howard and Lorraine Kingston
This bookstore features a good general selection with specialties in children's books and regional interest titles, along with autographed James Lee Burke titles.

Shadows-on-the-Teche Plantation
317 E. Main
New Iberia, LA 70560
(318) 369-6446
Open 9 A.M.–4:30 P.M. daily. Admission.

Shadows-on-the-Teche was originally built in 1834 by a sugarcane planter named David Weeks, who died before it was completed. His widow, who married Congressman John Moore, died there in 1863. The house was occupied by Union troops during the Civil War. Artist Weeks Hall, Mrs. Moore's great-grandson, made the restoration of the place his life's work; he died in 1958. Henry Miller described his visit to Shadows-on-the-Teche in *Air-Conditioned Nightmare*. While there, he signed Hall's famous kitchen door, which had also been autographed by such guests as Walt Disney, Cecil B. DeMille, D. W. Griffith, and H. L. Mencken.

New Roads

Point Coupee Museum and Tourist Center
8348 False River Rd.
New Roads, LA
(225) 638-7788
Thursday–Sunday, 11 A.M.–4 P.M. Admission.

This early Creole cottage once served as the home of Parlange Plantation workers. Pick up a brochure for a self-guided walking tour. This is Ernest Gaines country.

St. Francisville

Oakley House at Audubon State Park
11788 Highway 965
St. Francisville, LA 70775
(225) 635-3739

Each spring, the third weekend in March, the Audubon Pilgrimage recalls John James Audubon's visit to St. Francisville. He tutored the daughter of the Oakley House for a brief period, but was dismissed in disgrace. More an artist than a tutor, he painted thirty-two birds during those four months. There are many biographies of Audubon (Shirley Streshinsky's is the most recent), and Louisiana author John Gregory Brown is at work on a novel based on Audubon's stay at Oakley. For Pilgrimage information, call the West Feliciana Historical Society at (225) 635-6330.

St. Martinville

Evangeline statue
Town Square

Henry Wadsworth Longfellow's epic romantic poem about a fictional Acadian woman searching for her lost lover is part of local legend. There's a statue of Evangeline on the town square, near the famous Evangeline Oak. Check out the Petit Paris Museum and the Church of St. Martin de Tours.

Vacherie

Laura Plantation
2247 Highway 18
Vacherie, LA 70090
(225) 265-7690
9 A.M.–5 P.M. Admission.

Legend has it the famous Br'er Rabbit tales of Joel Chandler Harris had their origin in the Senegalese stories told by Laura Plantation slaves and in Creole folklore, collected by Alcée Fortier in his 1870 *Folktales of Louisiana.* For a lively modern adaptation of bayou folklore that will delight the whole family, read *With a Whoop and a Holler,* by Nancy Van Laan, illustrated by Scott Cook.

Oak Alley Plantation
3645 Highway 18
Vacherie, LA 70090
(225) 265-2151
Daily 9 A.M.–5:30 P.M. Admission.

The famous oak "allée," the double planted row of twenty-eight live oaks leading up to the entrance, is probably the most familiar plantation view in Louisiana. The Greek Revival house was built in 1839. Oak Alley appeared in the film adaptation of Anne Rice's novel *Interview with the Vampire.*

It's a funny thing how life can be such a drag one minute and a solid sender the next. The day I got out of jail Mardi Gras was being celebrated. It is a great day for all New Orleans, and particularly for the Zulu Aid Pleasure and Social Club. Every member of the Club masquerades in a costume burlesquing some famous person. The King of the Zulus, also in masquerade costume, rides with six other Zulus on a float giving away coconuts as souvenirs. The members march to the good jumping music of the brass bands while the King on his throne scrapes and bows to the cheering crowds. Every year, Mr. Jamke, the gravel and sand dealer, invites the King and his cortege and all the Zulus to come to his offices for champagne. He has been doing this as long as anyone can remember, and many of the Zulu members have been working for him ever since I was born.

When I ran into this celebration and the good music I forgot all about Sore Dick and the Parish Prison. Most of the members of the Zulu Club then lived around Liberty and Perdido Streets, but now Mardi Gras has become so famous—people come from all over America to see its parade—that it includes doctors, lawyers and other important people from all over the city. Later on a Lady Zulu Club was organized. It had been my life-long dream to be the King of the Zulus, as it was the dream of every kid in my neighborhood.

—Louis Armstrong, *Satchmo:*
My Life in New Orleans

Afterword

I remember the day I knew I could live happily in New Orleans. I had accompanied my husband here on a job interview, and during my free afternoon, I made the trek to Maple Street Book Shop. I bought a stack of books about New Orleans, and I particularly remember three: Sheila Bosworth's *Almost Innocent* (bookseller Rhoda Faust and I talked about the author's photograph on the jacket), Chris Wiltz's *Killing Circle,* and Valerie Martin's *Set in Motion.* (If you've read these books, you know that they aren't exactly the thing to set an anxious heart at rest, but they certainly tell you a lot about real life in New Orleans.) I set off down Maple Street, pleased with the prospect of books to read and a long streetcar ride on a beautiful day.

Then I heard my name being called and turned to find Rhoda rushing down the street after me. (Enterprising soul that she is, she'd read my name off the credit card slip.) As it turned out, Sheila Bosworth had just come in to the store and Rhoda introduced us. Sheila was gracious and signed my book, and we talked for a few minutes.

I left, feeling perfectly happy, thinking, "This is a town where you can just meet writers *on the street!*"

The literary charm of New Orleans, so perfectly captured in that exchange, the generosity of a writer and a bookseller toward an unknown reader, has never failed to sustain me. I spent my first year here reading books about New Orleans, reviewing books about New Orleans for the *Houston Post,* and discovering the city through the eyes of its writers. For the past ten years, as book review editor for the *Times-Picayune,* reading and writing about New Orleans writers has been my profession and my pleasure. Books about New Orleans and Louisiana fill my house and my heart. Books accompanied my family's exploration of our music and our food and the culture around us. Louisiana stories have been an important part of my children's upbringing.

The thrill of stepping into the fantasy is a big part of living here. At any minute you can become part of a parade, step into the big picture. So it was that my husband and I found ourselves at the 1988 Booklovers Ball, dancing on a riverboat on a foggy spring night, dressed as an eggplant and a streetcar in honor of Errol Laborde's book of New Orleans essays *I Never Danced with an Eggplant on a Streetcar Before*. We were surrounded by vampires and characters from Pat Conroy's *The Prince of Tides* (a lot of pretty girls with bandaged wrists), a remarkable tiger (who turned out to be novelist Tony Buchsbaum), and an Ignatius Reilly who stole the show (and no one ever found out who it was). It was one of those enchanted evenings that brought home to me how much New Orleanians love their books and writers.

When our children were young, we took them to that great literary treasure, Storyland in City Park, where nursery rhymes and fairy tales come to life. Last spring I had the pleasure of driving my teenaged daughter all over the city, from Faubourg Marigny to the French Quarter to Uptown, as she created a photo-essay based on sites associated with John Kennedy Toole's life and work.

I keep thinking back to the time mystery novelist Tony Dunbar told me, "You know, they say that nobody ever wrote anything great here." I've often pondered that remark, and tried to trace its source, for I disagree with it. Surely *A Streetcar Named Desire* will last, as will *The Moviegoer* and *A Confederacy of Dunces*. True, many of the finest books about New Orleans were written *from away,* as it were, as if the writers had to escape the city's spell in order to see it clearly and be able to write about. But that remark put me on notice to look for what is fine and enduring in writing about the city.

In ten years writing of about books for the *Times-Picayune,* I have watched the trajectory of literary careers with fascination. I have rejoiced when prestigious prizes were won, when big contracts were signed, and lamented the rest of the country's lack of appreciation of our talented writers. I have seen writers emerge and fade, arrive and depart.

To be sure, not all stories associated with the city have a happy ending. Someone once told me that if you have a flaw, New Orleans will exaggerate it. So we've lost writers—to drink and drugs and despair. New Orleans isn't exactly the place you go to straighten up if you're a writer; temptations are everywhere.

But for writers of all stripes, New Orleans provides a vital place to live and work, a chance to bump up against history every day and make a bit of it yourself. And those writers have made it a landscape beloved by readers. So many familiar stories have unfolded here. So many more are still to come. It has been my pleasure and my privilege to read them, to hear them, to spread the good word that literature remains alive and well in this enchanting, haunted city.

Winter passed and caterpillars began to cross the road again. I had spent a year in gathering and culling over folk-tales. I loved it, but I had to bear in mind that there was a limit to the money to be spent on the project, and as yet, I had done nothing about hoodoo. So I slept a night, and the next morning I headed my toenails toward Louisiana. . . .

New Orleans is now and has ever been the hoodoo capital of America. Great names in rites that vie with those of Hayti in deeds, that keep alive the powers of Africa.

Hoodoo, or Voodoo, as pronounced by the whites, is burning with a flame in America, with all the intensity of a suppressed religion. It has its thousands of secret adherents. It adapts itself like Christianity to its locale, reclaiming some of its borrowed characteristics to itself. Such as fire-worship as signified in the Christian church by the altar and the candles. And the belief in the power of water to sanctify as in baptism.

Belief in magic is older than writing. So nobody knows how it started.

—Zora Neale Hurston, *Mules and Men*